CREATIVITY SUCKS

CREATIVITY SUCKS

SUCKS

>»>» «««

PHIL HANSEN

A TarcherPerigee Book

. . . AND 30 OTHER THINGS I'VE LEARNED WHILE LIVING A WEIRD, AMAZING, CRAZY, CREATIVE LIFE (LIKE THE FACT THAT SUCCESS CAN KILL YOUR CREATIVITY, LIMITATIONS CAN BE GOOD, AND IF YOU WANT TO MAKE A LIVING AS A CREATIVE PROFESSIONAL, DON'T SIT AROUND WAITING FOR THE "PERFECT" MOMENT BECAUSE THERE'S NEVER A CONVENIENT TIME TO DITCH REALITY AND CHASE YOUR DREAMS. SO, FLIP OR READ DEEP, START YOUR JOURNEY TO EXPLORE THIS PATH, OR GO FULL-ON AND TAKE THE GIANT LEAP, ASSURED THAT I TOO HAVE EXPERIENCED EVERY UP AND DOWN OF THIS MARVELOUS, AGONIZING, EXCITING LIFE, AND I WILL ACCOMPANY YOU SO YOU'RE NOT ALL ALONE IN THIS SOLITARY PURSUIT TO TAKE WHAT'S IN YOUR IMAGINATION AND MAKE IT YOUR LIFE.)

tarcherperigee

An imprint of Penguin Random House LLC
penguinrandomhouse.com

TarcherPerigee with tp colophon is a registered trademark of Penguin Random House LLC

Most TarcherPerigee books are available at special quantity discounts for bulk purchase for sales promotions, premiums, fund-raising, and educational needs. Special books or book excerpts also can be created to fit specific needs. For details, write: SpecialMarkets@penguin randomhouse.com.

Library of Congress Cataloging-in-Publication Data

Names: Hansen, Phil, author.
Title: Creativity sucks: and 30 other things I've learned while living a
weird, amazing, crazy, creative life / by Phil Hansen.
Description: New York: TarcherPerigee, LLC, 2020.
Identifiers: LCCN 2020005296 | ISBN 9780143131526 (hardcover)
Subjects: LCSH: Creative ability. | Self-actualization (Psychology)
Classification: LCC BF408 .H38656 2020 | DDC 153.3/5—dc23
LC record available at https://lccn.loc.gov/2020005296
p.   cm.

Printed in the United States of America
10   9   8   7   6   5   4   3   2   1

Book design by Tiffany Estreicher

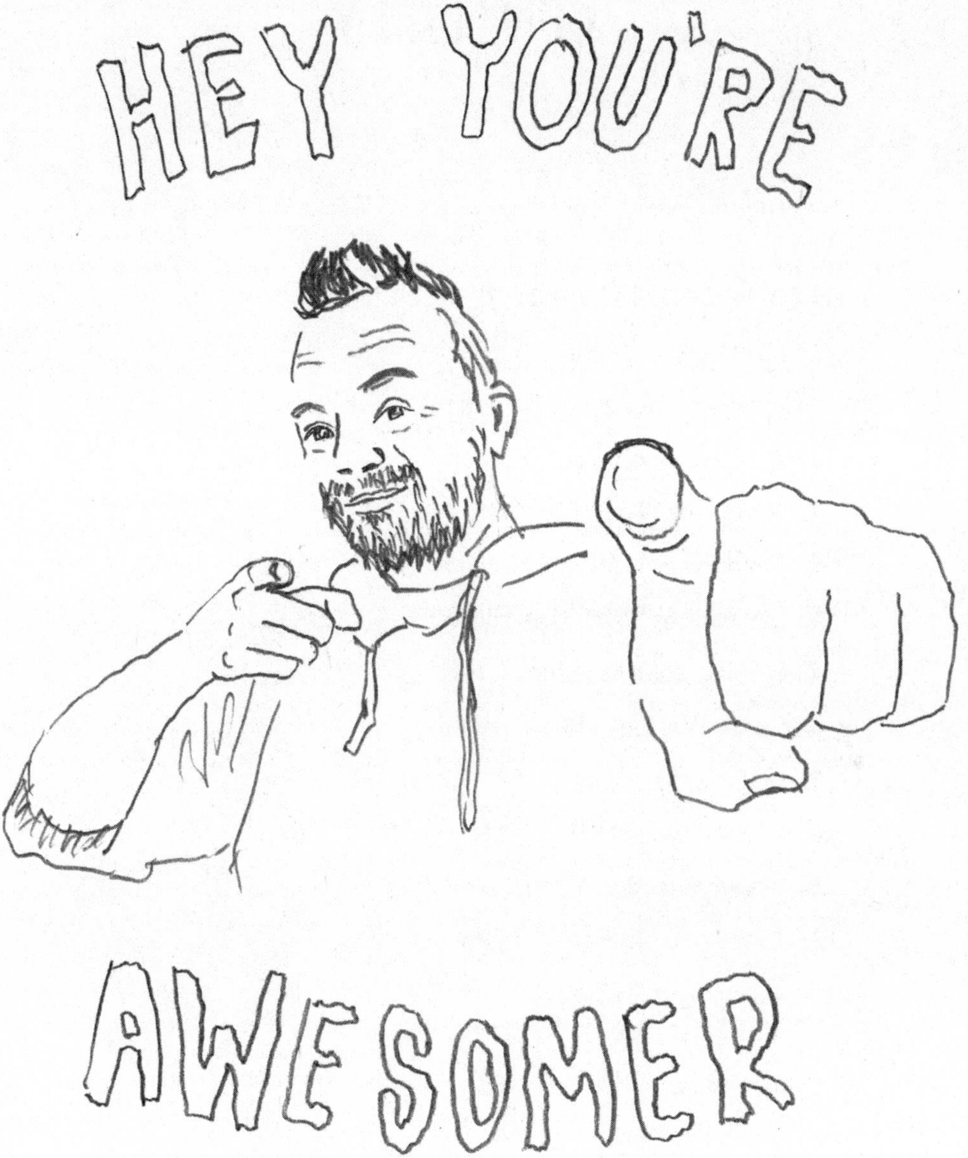
HEY YOU'RE
AWESOMER

CONTENTS

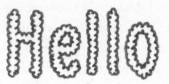

Creativity sucks, but if you're anything like me, you might already know that. The long days; the thought-filled, sleepless nights; the judgment and criticism that may come not only from strangers—not only from loved ones (eesh)—but also from yourself. And that's not even touching what it's like when you try to earn an income from it.

In this book, I'm brutally honest about the hard times I've faced as a professional artist making a living, a name, and works that have made some people see things in their world differently. Despite the way "creative success" can often appear to the outside world, some of the moments can be a little dark, a little lonely, and filled with a lot of questions. I've found that with support from my loved ones, an ever-thickening skin against critics, and a some-times foolishly enduring commitment to my passion, I've always managed to make it to the other side stronger, more determined, more adaptable, and often even more skilled than I was before.

I know you can relate because we all use creativity. Whether for our job or as a hobby, each of us accesses some level of creativity every single day, in fields ranging from engineering and entrepreneurship to the world of art.

Primarily, this book is for people who want to express that creativity through art like writing, dancing, music, sculpting, design, cartooning, filmmaking, YouTubing, or photography. But much of the advice here can also be applied across a range of environments: maybe you're looking for a solution to a problem at your day job. You could be cooking some exotic meal at home. You could even be working on a portrait of Edgar Allan Poe fashioned out of worms (I'll explain). Our generation is embracing creativity like no generation before, and this is amplifying the impact each of us has on the world. It's insane and infectious.

On the other hand, it's also a lot to navigate. That's especially true today, in a time when a budding artist can ask themselves: *How am I going to live off of my art when sales/views/likes/[insert other uncontrollable outcome here] are so subjective, but also necessary?* If it seems tougher than ever to step up and express your individuality, your observation is on point. But shouldn't you use that fear for fuel?

Over the years, as I've spoken with lots of people who do what I do (as well as those who are curious about it), I've picked up on some interesting themes, insights, and "rules" about the creative life. These pages are filled with those perspectives, along with a few of my oddball opinions and probably at least one idea that will leave you questioning my sense of reality.

Throughout this book, I examine this life through the three

main facets I believe any artist should focus on: ideas, motivation, and skills. Then I break the book down into three segments that follow the artist's journey:

1. **More Than the Big Toe**, or what's necessary for you to fully commit yourself to a creative life path

2. **Finding Your Flow**, on establishing a solid everyday routine

3. **Keep On Keeping On**, or staying motivated and continuing to grow your skills and approach, even after you've reached some of your biggest goals

This third part is what a lot of my cohorts and I have had to work the hardest to acquire. The way the world changes is the reason we have to keep creating. As our society grows more and more automated, we all should learn to think more innovatively, more resourcefully . . . more creatively. Nobody said living an artful life is easy. But I say it's worth your while.

Because here's the deal: bringing creativity into your life is easy. Keeping it, however, is not. On the road ahead are periods of isolation, days spent struggling to come up with ideas, times when your most brilliant execution goes totally underrated, and moments of failure—plain and simple. So, why do we even bother?

We choose creativity because it leads to amazing glory, times when ideas will flood through you with an energy that rattles you, times when you will be lauded for your creative work, and times of magnificent achievement when you'll find you've touched people's lives and transformed how humans think. We choose creativity because for the true creative person, not sharing what's inside us just doesn't feel like an option.

If you're longing to make your creative passion more front and center in your life, I wrote this book to equip you with more perspective, tips, and revelations. Creativity can be a grind, my friends . . . but that's just part of what makes it so damn beautiful.

—phil

p.s. Be sure to draw a picture of
      yourself here so we can start
      this book on the same page.

Part 1

More Than the Big Toe

1

Creativity Sucks

Several years ago, I found myself totally depressed at what was arguably the highest point in my career. It was a very strange time. To the outside world, I was riding high on success . . . but on the inside, I was in an emotional gutter. I had just given a TED Talk, starred in a commercial for Mazda that aired throughout Europe, created a commissioned piece for the Rockefeller Foundation that was displayed in the middle of Times Square, and launched an art education startup. If it sounds cool, I suppose it was. Since I was a kid, I'd worked so hard to reach that point, and I'd always expected it would make me incredibly happy. Oddly, it didn't.

All the while, I kept waiting for it to set in—that feeling that I'd arrived. Sure, at times it would hit me: *Wow, check out my life!* But those moments didn't last. Instead, over a period of a few months, I realized I had never been more depressed. I gained thirty pounds, developed some facial tics, and started drinking so much that it dawned on me that I was becoming an alcoholic. At thirty-four years old, I'd managed to send my blood pressure through the roof. When you're your own boss, you don't have to call in sick; and one morning when I woke up after a few too many the night before, it occurred to me that I was turning into the stereotypical artist: a deadbeat depressive drunk. And maybe I was.

I was deflated. Confused. While I was living what others had labeled "the dream," creativity was revealing itself to me like a stranger the morning after a one-night stand: now that the magic had happened, I was seeing that it also had an ugly side. It was like the part of my identity that I'd always been able to count on—the impulse to create that had made me who I was—had turned on me. At that point, I learned something completely unexpected about a topic I thought I knew a lot about: *creativity has the potential to completely suck.*

Sucking comes in various forms, like . . .

» We can't control when our ideas come to us, if they come at all. (Grr.)

» Our goal may be to create something original, but dang, it seems so hard to be original anymore.

» When we make a living from our creativity, that often makes us less creative.

» There is rarely enough time or money to complete our moonshot projects.

» Even when we spend a ton of effort on something, it still might get tossed.

» Our ideas could be great, but we may not have the skills to bring them to life.

» The stress of executing a project can diminish any enjoyment we feel.

» Dealing with our inner critic and other people's opinions honestly really hurts sometimes.

The creative trajectory is so different from how progress is measured in other fields. When we look at how our society treats

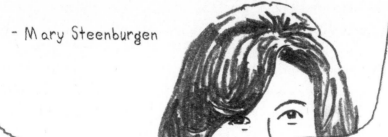

When you're young people say to you, "You can do anything, try playing a musical instrument, try learning a foreign language." And then there's some point where no one says that to you and then, worse, you don't say it to yourself.

- Mary Steenburgen

the feats that we can quantify (think: a career in sports with a high salary, millions of fans, ESPN highlight shows, and special recognition), most people are coached to reach these achievements in a completely different way than any creative goal. When a kid learns a sport, adults tell him or her: "No pain, no gain!" or "When the going gets tough, the tough get going!" From a young age, we inherently understand that it's going to take a ton of effort before we can pump our chests with pride on the playing field. But no one tells us about the grit that creativity takes. Painting? Photography? It's perceived as fun, fun, fun. In reality, you and I both know these endeavors take endurance and perseverance. They require the same discipline and dedication that sports do: getting to it early, training and practice, muscle memory, falls and flops—just like in any area of study or work where success is determined quantitatively.

Maybe that's why, historically, art has been taken less seriously than something like sports. It shouldn't surprise any of us that very few high school graduates pursue a creative outlet, and fewer still will go on to pursue a career in the arts. It's because we're not raised to deal with the type of difficulty that comes along with it. When we finger-paint in preschool, Mom hangs it on the fridge. When we're in college, the professor gives us assignments in which to create and we get a grade. Later, when we're responsible for generating one original idea after another and our career depends on it, we may think we're in over our heads. When we hit a rough patch, it's probable many of us are not quite prepared to weather the storm. On top of that, once our childhood cheering sections dissipate and we struggle with our creativity, people say things like, "I sure hope you have a backup plan" or the clichéd classic: "Better keep your day job!"

After my TED Talk, the TV ad campaign, and everything else that had happened by the time I reached the height of my career and the lowest of my spirits, I accepted that creativity can (and often does) suck. I stopped parroting "It's supposed to be *fun!*" and instead started discussing it with my peers. When we all got real and acknowledged that we were not total masters 100 percent of the time, I noticed that my misery was not all that uncommon.

First of all, it seemed like no one wanted to talk about it because a lot of the accomplished artists I knew didn't want to give off the appearance that great work doesn't always flow naturally. Keeping up that mask was a burden in and of itself, but once we broke through it, the list of struggles ran the gamut: from waiting to get paid by clients (and knowing what kind of price tag to put on our work) to listening to the harsh opinions of people who aren't as familiar with art—working in this world comes with a lot of in-

No one but myself knows the anxiety I go through and the trouble I give myself to finish paintings...

- Monet

herent fights. It turns out feeling defeated from time to time is a universal truth for any individual who lives his, her, or their life guided by a creative passion.

As I write this, it's finally crystal clear to me that every creative I know has been beaten and bruised by the art life—and yet, we still love it. Why? Because the greatest skill we all share is having the strength to weather the tough times and hang on. The good times will return for things to click and make sense again. So, that's why I do this. Yep, that's why. Because as much as creativity sucks sometimes, what will actually define your success are the times you bounce back, push through, and keep moving forward.

The first step to the rest of your journey is to accept that the artist's life is not all puppy dogs and paintbrushes. Oh, you'll have the honeymoon moments, the hits, the highs, the high fives. But then shit will get real in a jiffy. Even if you've never experienced it, it happens to the best of us.

2

How Creativity Sucks (You In)

We're one chapter deep, and we've already covered a fine plethora of ways creativity can stump us. So, why are we the ones who have been lured by the call to the awesome but unpredictable creative life? Is there a trait we makers all share?

There is. By the time you've picked up this book, you've already placed value on your creativity. You've set it above other activities; you've determined it deserves your investment—your time, your attention, sometimes even your money. An individual with creativity is someone who will choose working on a project over kicking up their feet and watching a show. They'll consider bypassing brunch with friends to spend that time learning a new skill, or they'll use that block of free time to make progress on a project. This is *awesome* because it's something any of us can do right now. When we reach the point where any others are actually starting to show interest in our art, it's because we were the ones who first deemed our work worthwhile. I should add that usually even before that phase, there's a process of discernment when our dabbling turns into decision.

For me, the path to a creative life was straightforward at first. Growing up, I liked drawing and art as much as most of my peers did, but in high school, my interest reached a new level. I had an art teacher (shout-out to Mr. Phelan) who supported creativity in general above any specific "skill." He encouraged me to follow my imagination into whatever my curiosity was.

For a Pacific Northwestern kid with a lot of inquisitiveness and energy, that was all I needed to hear. Mr. Phelan probably didn't even know it at the time, but he gave me permission to explore my interests in a way that transported me outside of my everyday world. I grew very focused, spending a lot of time drawing and developing my skill set. The truth is, I didn't have any natural talent. Seriously. I just worked my butt off to get better. These days my product seems more effortless because

IF YOU ENJOY IT, KEEP DOING IT; AND WHEN YOU GET BORED, PUSH YOUR OWN BOUNDARIES.

I put in the time back then, but to a certain extent it amuses me to remember that kid who had no clue what he was doing but was so hungry to keep doing it.

That's how creativity is: we have no idea where it will take us, but we dream and go where it leads. It took me years to get any good at drawing. Today, if someone were to analyze my work from back then, they would see that I had some flair in terms of my inventiveness, but I wasn't good. There are thousands of people with far better raw talent. Back then, I was just willing to work—and these days, I just keep working, nudging at the boundaries, looking for holes to poke and places to expand.

Recently, I was chatting with an acquaintance who used to draw cartoons for our college paper, but he hasn't done much with it since. "How did you just keep making stuff?" he asked me. The way he asked seemed to suggest that he felt some regret for not having stayed the course. I told him what Mr. Phelan taught me: if you enjoy it, keep doing it; and when you get bored, push your own boundaries. Art drew me in through a desire to see something I've created take on a life beyond myself. I do this because it's how I share. The aspiration for creative expression isn't just for the young. You know you're meant for this life when nobody else can talk you out of it.

3

Avoid
the Squeeze

You've seen it—and if you haven't, you will: that phase in life when the creative pursuits of the people you know are squeezed out of their lives. "The squeeze" usually begins as "life things" stacked up, like a full-time job, a relationship, a home to take care of, and other responsibilities. Don't be that artist who one day looks up from your corporate desk or your cool new car and realizes that your creative projects have been simmering on the back burner for years. We all intend to get back to making art as soon as things calm down and we get a little window to focus on a project, but guess

what? Life never stops happening. You are the only one who can carve out that time.

When a friend of mine began art school, her professor dropped this classic scare tactic on her class. "Look to your left," he said. "Now look to your right. After you graduate, half of you won't be making art." My friend felt there was no way that she or her friends would ever fall into that trap. Art was her life. But when I ran into her two years after graduation . . . you guessed it. She was working full-time as a clerk in a law office. She'd completely stopped making art. So had many of her friends, and she only knew one person from her entire class who was making a living from their art.

LIFE NEVER STOPS HAPPENING.

The squeeze is natural. Art alone is work, and making a living from it takes some serious hustle. There are so many highly trained and talented artists who realized: hey, life is easier when you can count on the basics—especially a regular paycheck. Valid? Absolutely. But creating is such an important part of the artist's identity that if he or she is not expressing what's inside them, they don't feel totally alive. That's why I hear lots of older folks say, "I wish I had kept doing art my whole life!" Waiting to take a sculpture class at the senior center makes for a lot of years of not living fully.

There's a solution to that: don't ever stop. The world will always threaten to squeeze the creativity out of our lives. You've got to set proper expectations; you've got to hold that space in your life and protect it. It makes you who you are.

I've observed a few beliefs that creative people hold about how easily their careers will go, and how these beliefs can impact an artist's future:

1. It Will Be Easy. This is Darwin's natural selection of the creative world. Thinking the masses will gobble up your work right out of the gate will squeeze out a sizable cohort of your colleagues. A lot of developing artists expect to graduate and stumble straight into lucrative art careers and full-time creative jobs, not to mention all the creature comforts that go with being a raving success. If you fall into this mindset, and you're not striking it rich in your field yet . . . maybe you need to seek out another perspective. Forget making a million dollars from your art. Simply having your art in your life as you age is an accomplishment to marvel. If you find yourself thinking it will be easy, eventually you'll need to choose between letting your creative projects slide or hunkering down and working harder.

2. Hard Work Will Get Me There. This type of person believes their creativity comes before other things in life.

They won't talk about lowercase "plan b" much (if ever), but they do have it, just in case everything falls apart. Plan b might mean getting a roommate or getting a day job if the money runs out. But they aren't giving up their art for anything. It won't be easy, but if you can adopt this attitude and really stick to it, your art career can survive for years before feeling a serious squeeze.

3. Suffering Is Expected. This type of mindset is the most likely to "make it" because they understand that a ton of hard work, along with the alignment of some stars, is usually involved when trying to make a living from art. This artist type will wait patiently for an opportunity to strike and keep their living costs way down while honing their craft.

Looking back, the second belief and a day job were how I managed to live a creative life. I knew from a young age that it would be tough to make a direct living from my art. So, for many years I worked as an X-ray tech. It allowed me to make decent money while also giving me enough days off each week that I could pour into my artwork, work in all the different ways I wanted to explore, and not be tied to the sale of my work. For years, I ate frozen burritos for dinner, didn't have a car, and even moved halfway across the country to live in my brother's basement so I could continue focusing on my art.

If you want to keep from getting your art life squeezed, these are the kinds of sacrifices you'll have to make. Live as frugally as

TIME → MINDSET	FRESH OUT OF SCHOOL	FEELING SOME HARDSHIP OVER HERE	THE SHITTY TIMES HAVE ARRIVED	ALL HELL IS BREAKING LOOSE
IT'S GOING TO BE EASY	Here I come, bitches! #artlife	This wasn't in the brochure.	I work in an office now.	Bailed a long time ago.
HARD WORK WILL GET ME THERE	All right, let's get this adventure started.	Not what I had hoped for, but it's okay, I got this.	Daaaaaamn.	Engaging backup plan!
SUFFERING IS EXPECTED	Holding on to some of my student loans to make a nest egg was a good place to start.	This is expected.	I will not get squeezed out. I've prepared for this.	I'm settling in for the ride. One day this will make a good story.

possible, put aside some cash, and find time that you can spend completely on your craft.

As we get older, the squeeze (read: *reality*) closes in even more. It will be our mindset, not our talent, that determines if our art can survive that conflict. Stop feeling pressure to be like all the people you see on Instagram. I have a feeling that's not your style anyway.

If you weigh all this and decide the starving artist path isn't for you, I won't judge. I promise. And remember: at any point in your life, you can decide to recommit to your art and change course. For those of you who are out there scratching and clawing to find a way to live the art life, *you are my heroes.* The material world isn't going anywhere. These days, just the thought of a frozen burrito gives me instant indigestion, but I'm still standing. If you love your art more than anything in the world, don't be like the pack. The ability to endure the squeeze will set you apart from the rest.

Jay was 29 and I was 25 and we were living in Austin. And you know it's like kinda cute when you're 18 and 22 going out to pursue the arts and all of our friends in high school were like "that's so cool." Now it was fucking sad and depressing and our parents were scared and they were starting to have those serious conversations with us about when we were going to give this up.

- Mark Duplass

4

Most Ideas Are Shit

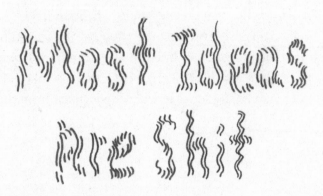

The moment we first gaze upon a mind-blowing work of art, it can feel like we're in the presence of something magical—something that was snatched out of the cosmic ether. *Wow*, we muse. *How'd they come up with that?* The next question automatically being: *And why didn't I come up with that?* If you're a creative person, sometimes (often/always) it can be particularly frustrating to witness others around you coming up with amazing ideas when it feels so difficult to come up with groundbreaking new inspiration of your own. If you're wondering, *How did they dream that up?*, well, here's a little secret about us creative folk: most of our ideas are actually shit.

I hope you find that little nugget comforting. Here's the deal: most artists know that generating boatloads of ideas before they strike that special one is a process—always. On the rare occasion, instant cosmic strokes of genius do happen, but by and large, we

Ideas don't just come full blown from your head, you grind them out, you discover them. I think it's why I've been a professional writer since 1982 and my first drafts still suck. And the reason I don't get upset is because it's not an act of creation, it's an act of discovery.

- Nell Scovell

humans tend to have far more bad ideas than good ones. It's why painters fill sketchbooks, bands jam, writers edit, and dancers practice moving in a million different ways. It's why paper tears so easily out of a notebook and why the delete button exists. On occasion (frequent occasion), all of us scrap something that just wasn't working and start all over on something that feels more certain.

I invite you to grasp this as a fundamental rule. Otherwise it would be too easy for any of us to be scared off from pursuing a creative career. If you live with the assumption that artists don't struggle, please allow this book to convince you otherwise.

Your weapon here is in the volume of ideas you come up with.

You need to cultivate new ideas constantly, all while working to improve the universal quality of the work you conjure up. Absorb feedback from mentors, colleagues, and friends in the know, but most of all, listen to your own inner wisdom. Often, we can sense for ourselves that a specific concept needs a little more thought, work, or time to evolve. And if all your ideas are piles of crap? That's still gold! Just toss them on the compost heap and circle back to them later. I do it all the time.

If most ideas are shit (and they are), then be prepared to work, scrap, adjust, and adapt. You'll know an idea has potential when you sit on it but keep coming back around to it—when it just won't leave you alone. In the end, your creation may appear to have been pulled from thin air. While people around you ooh and aah, you can smile, quietly appreciating the time you put in.

5

Creative Evolution

A few years ago, a juice company was interested in hiring me to create a project for an ad campaign. Thrilled at the prospect, I tested out a few quick concepts and decided to pitch an idea where I'd take a large horizontal sheet of glass and glue on plastic dividers to create the framework that would turn the glass into a liquid canvas, or a coloring book of sorts. Then I would pour different-colored fruit juices into a bunch of cordoned-off cavities to form this giant, juicy image. It was going to be so visual, so thirst-invoking, so awesome . . . I can still taste the juice just thinking about it. That's why I was surprised when the company didn't go for it.

I refused to dump the concept down the drain, so I composted it . . . for six freaking years. That's when one day, I was listening to the radio and heard Snoop Dogg come on, singing "Gin and Juice." *Whoa*, I thought. I could add gin to my idea and create a

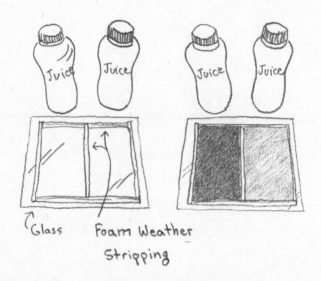

Glass Foam Weather Stripping

picture of Snoop. It wound up an even cooler concept than the one I'd pitched to the juice brand. With help, plastic borders were placed to create a big, portrait-sized mold, then I used different-colored juices and juice concentrates mixed with gin to convey the features and contours in Snoop's face. This project sat on my compost heap for years, and when it finally came to life it was glorious. I kept waiting for Snoop to share the video. That would've been amazing. He didn't, but who knows, maybe next year!

Like any good entertainer, few artists will tell you that the perfectly presented piece you're staring at actually started out as a confounding clump of curiosity and only developed into something noteworthy *over time*—but that's almost always the case. Peel back the curtain on any creative person's process, and you'll find dozens of steps (and missteps) that went into conceiving, molding, cutting (sometimes, yes, cursing), shaping, and reshaping an idea—for weeks, months, *years even*—until one day that little idea flourished into an astounding work of art. It's possible that

the artist doesn't even realize all the incremental effort that went into it if they work intuitively, so once it all comes together it can feel like magic, even to the artist.

Don't buy it? "But some of our most iconic songs were reportedly pulled from thin air!" you might say. Well, yeah. The White Stripes wrote "Seven Nation Army" during a sound check. Kanye wrote "All Falls Down" in fifteen minutes. Paul McCartney beat them both to it when he wrote "Yesterday" in ten minutes. Of course inspiration can happen in a flash for artists who constantly create and have the level of skill and motivation to run with an idea once it strikes. But those are outliers, even for the greats. What I know is that most art does not come from the divine. It almost always comes from a lot of hard work and many, many trial runs.

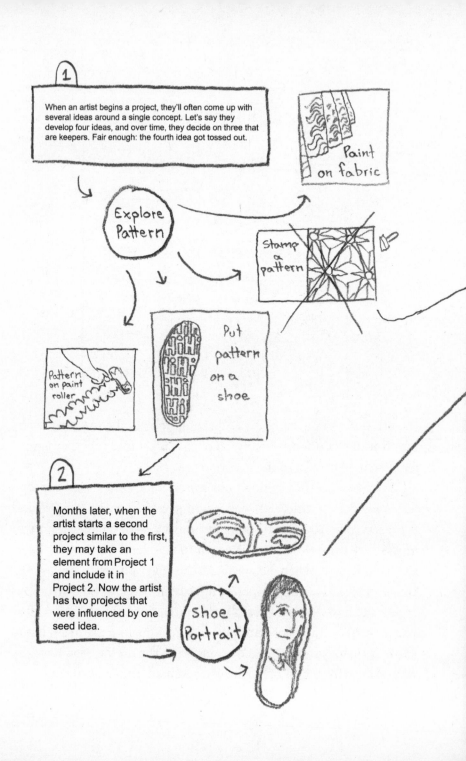

1

When an artist begins a project, they'll often come up with several ideas around a single concept. Let's say they develop four ideas, and over time, they decide on three that are keepers. Fair enough: the fourth idea got tossed out.

Paint on fabric

Explore Pattern

Stamp a pattern

Pattern on paint roller

Put pattern on a shoe

2

Months later, when the artist starts a second project similar to the first, they may take an element from Project 1 and include it in Project 2. Now the artist has two projects that were influenced by one seed idea.

Shoe Portrait

3

A few weeks later, the artist may look back at the fourth shitty idea they tossed away from Project 1 and get inspired to combine it with a variation of the Project 2 idea.

Portrait with stamp

4

This creative cross-pollination happens again and again in an artist's life. It's why we must keep tabs on those amazing shitty ideas!

In the end, we the people only get to see the final step in the evolution of an idea that's been in the artist's head for ages. It may cause our brains to explode, but to the artist? Nothing incredible happened. They just followed the steps in their process to get to that point. Now that you've seen how strangely circuitous the creative evolution process can be, try to be gentler on yourself the next time you're stuck. Shelve it, go on a walk, and return tomorrow or next year. There are a lot of components in the universe that need to line up for expert artistic execution. Having that patience for your process is a special skill that develops with experience.

You have to be willing to give your ideas time to breathe, morph, and evolve. Fairly recently I posted a picture of Edgar Allan Poe that I'd made with seven thousand worms. I constructed it on the ground and filmed the worms as they crawled away. Then I reversed the video so the worms appeared to come from nowhere and make the portrait. It had a little viral action online and people were impressed with the originality. But did I tell people I had done worm art before? No, they thought I just came up with it. They were blown away.

A quick version of the backstory goes like this: a long time ago, I was on a walk after a spring rain. I realized I was dodging all the worms on the ground (since a care for nature is often another trait among us who create art). First, I thought it would be a good idea to collect them and go fishing the next day. Then I thought, *Wait: would it be possible to collect enough worms to make some weird artwork with them?* I started thinking about it and came up with a handful of ideas. The most practical of them was to make a hollow mold in a specific shape and dump them in. Then when I removed the mold, the worms would be lying on the paper in the same shape.

I did that and created a picture of a bird! Too on the beak for you? Well, the reaction from myself and people online was mixed, and I eventually deleted the video that I had posted. But all was not lost, because I'd figured out how to make a picture with a living, moving medium like worms, which was a totally new skill for me. It hadn't been about anything sophisticated, like the juxtaposition between slime and beauty. More than anything, I just wanted to see whether it could be done.

Then a few years later I did it again—this time with more production and an even harder-hitting concept. I made four images of different fears I have in life: lacking money, death, having children, and the future of humanity. That, too, faded away without much attention. But by the time I developed Poe at the third iteration, I'd hit on both a concept and powerful visual that really clicked for a mass audience. Edgar Allan Poe was known to be macabre, and there's something about worms that makes a lot of people's skin crawl. I'd hit on a combination that people wanted to share. It took years for the original idea to evolve to this point, but I was patient with myself and accepted that the first couple of stabs were just part of the process.

What's the lesson? Keep a running list of your good and bad ideas. I have years' worth of online files, notes on my phone, physical pieces of paper, and notes in drawing books of different ideas I have for projects. Every once in a while, I take out the ones that still interest me and put them on a piece of paper, which I tape to the wall inside a giant funnel I drew. The projects start at the top of the funnel with many others, and as I work on them, they move closer to the end of the funnel.

And if a project gets started, but I wane on it, I'll put a note on the card then bump it back to the top of the funnel.

So, don't trash an idea. Put it in your compost pile or funnel and see if it gains new life at another point. Even when you think an idea is teetering on disaster, trust the process. Ideas need a lot of love and support to grow and evolve. And when they do, trust that they will coalesce into something profound, beautiful, and uniquely you.

You write a book and it takes you forever and you make all kinds of mistakes and then you finally figure out what you are doing. Then you go back and take out all of the worst mistakes, the ones that you can find, and you make it look like you knew what you were doing all along. That's the final illusion.

- Richard Russo

6

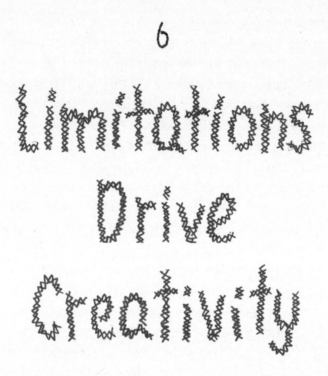

Limitations Drive Creativity

Our society does a great job at inspiring, encouraging, and sometimes even demanding that individuals today dream big and maintain our uniqueness as we plan out how we'll live our lives. I've fallen for it, too—I even spent years of my life pushing myself to think as originally as I possibly could anytime I was working to come up with an art project. But what I seem to learn over and over again is that the grand, super-original ideas I had that were truly outside the box were also so far outside my realm of possibility that they were almost useless to me. Sure, the ideas might have been slick and original, but they completely ignored the realities of my life. Either they took too much time to create while I had a full-time job to contend with, or they cost too much money to bring to life while I had bills to pay. As great as these big ideas were, they didn't fit within the constraints of my life ... so at a certain point, I began to resist the idea of thinking wildly outside the box. *Screw thinking outside of it,* I thought. *That's not my world. I need my creative ideas to thrive inside the reality of my life.*

At this point, I made a small mental shift that continues to have huge implications on my life and creativity. I decided: instead of trying to shoot for the crazy huge idea and waiting months or years to do so, why not focus my creativity to work with what I have, and literally use the limitations of my life to push me creatively?

When I realized this, it took my work to a transcendent place.

It's so easy to view our limitations as though they're blocking us from achieving our creative goals. A lack of time or not enough money are legit reasons for feeling constrained—but what if your limitations really can be a source of your creativity? I've seen it happen in my own life; my TED Talk a while back was based on this concept. I spoke of the struggles and sadness of a dream lost, followed by the elation of discovering that our limitations can be one of our greatest assets.

The moment I walked off the stage at that talk, people began to ask me how they could embrace their own limitations. I'll be honest: I couldn't advise them. My only explanation was that my ability to live my life doing what I loved depended on my willingness to completely reframe how I thought about struggle. Here's the story.

Years ago, when I was still in high school, my right hand started shaking, and it was getting progressively worse. The shake had developed because I was obsessed with pointillism, also called stippling. This is a technique in which an artist employs a bunch of tiny dots to create a greater cohesive image. An iconic example is Georges Seurat's *A Sunday on La Grande Jatte*, which lives at the Art Institute of Chicago (and which you may have seen in the 1980s movie *Ferris Bueller's Day Off*). Pointillism was my jam. It was the type of meticulous, detailed work that I still love today.

As I spent more and more time meticulously placing thousands of tiny dots on a page with a pen, I began to notice a tremor developing in my hand. It started naturally, probably from being jacked up on caffeine or lacking sleep (which was pretty routine for me in high school). It wasn't presenting itself as a problem anywhere else in my life . . . but when my hand shook while doing pointillism, it totally screwed up the images. To compensate for the shake, I started to hold my pen extremely tightly—which only compounded the problem. Constantly battling the shake took its toll: before long, my hand began to shake even when I wasn't creating art.

Eventually, my right hand shook all day, every day. I thought my art career was over before it began, and I was devastated. Disheartened, disillusioned, and destroyed—all that—I ended up dropping out of art school, and I quit making art entirely.

Then a few years later, a friend asked to see some of my old drawings. When I showed her, she encouraged me to start creating again. It took a little convincing, but I knew I'd been missing my art a ton. I hadn't picked up my sketchbook in years, but the minute I opened it up, I felt a swell of energy return that I hadn't sensed for a while. I started messing around with some drawings and was expecting to be worse than I was years before, but I was pleasantly surprised to see the total opposite: I was even better than I was before. This was exciting, and I began drawing a little in my spare time . . . but the tremor still affected everything I did.

I decided to find out what the shake was all about, so I made an appointment with a neurologist. He put me through some different tests and sighed in that way no patient wants to hear. "Well," he said, "it looks like the shake is permanent."

I was stunned.

As I tuned back into the conversation, he explained that I had spent so much time holding my pen so tightly that my brain no longer knew what it was to hold my hand truly steady. There were no two ways about it. "Your hand is going to shake for the rest of your life," the doctor said.

It was like being a hairstylist with carpal tunnel who can't hold scissors or a comb; a chef who can't chop because of arthritis in the wrists. Who would I be if I couldn't make art? What the hell would I do with the rest of my life?

As if he could hear my thoughts while I sat slumped in the chair, the doctor did something a little unexpected: he chimed in with advice. "Why don't you just embrace the shake?" he said.

Huh?

For a second, I thought he was being sarcastic, dismissive . . . until I glanced up at his face. He was being really sincere. Still, it wasn't the advice I wanted to hear (at all), so I rose from the chair and exited the exam room in a daze.

A few weeks later, I was riding the bus, still bummed out and thinking about the neurologist's words. That's when I began to wonder: *Could I really find a way to make art with the shake? What if I took his advice literally?*

When I got home, I pinned a piece of paper to the wall. Then I grabbed a pencil and started to draw. I didn't try to control the shake. I let my hand go wild, shaking and scribbling with every stroke. I played with the scribbles, toying around to see if there was some way I could make them work for me. I made light shades, dark shades, gradients, and so on. I was actually starting to see some interesting results, so I began drawing pictures with just scribbles. And it was at this point that I felt something I hadn't felt in years: happiness. Drawing with scribbles felt liberating. It made me laugh because it felt so silly to create art this way—and even sillier that I hadn't just tried it before. Unbeknownst to me, what I'd thought would be a career killer was about to transform how I explored every facet of creativity.

I began to experiment with other ways of making art. I missed pointillism and contemplated why I liked it so much. It was because there was such a magic, such a satisfaction, in stepping back from all those little dots to marvel at the completeness of an image made of fragments. Those little specks each contributed to something grand and powerful.

So, I tried messing around with making fragmented pictures, essentially using different materials as individual dots. This exploration led me to work with nontraditional materials—like painting with my feet, burning wood with a blowtorch, or grinding away at wood with power tools. Because of my physical limitation, I found myself exploring the far reaches of my imagination. I had embraced my shake, and that choice led me to discover so much more about my potential.

The idea even crossed my mind that if limitations would push me creatively, then maybe I needed to create limitations for myself. I started small by rethinking the paintbrush. Why use one? I'll use something else! I happened to watch a movie on basic cable that weekend that gave me the idea to use my hands to paint a picture. The following week, I was busy at work: I dipped my hands in paint and karate chopped a picture of Bruce Lee.

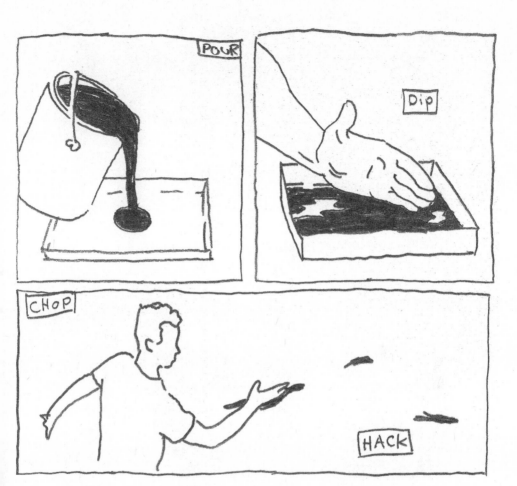

Utilizing limitations pushed me into some of the strangest places, like painting thirty pictures on my stomach of people or things that influenced me. Or to present myself with the ultimate limitation—destroying my art. This project was comprised of twenty-three different pieces that were created and then destroyed, including a sculpture of Jimi Hendrix made with matches that I set on fire after it was completed. When a friend asked me what this represented to me, my answer was clear: nothing! Through what my art was communicating to my audience, I was learning not to

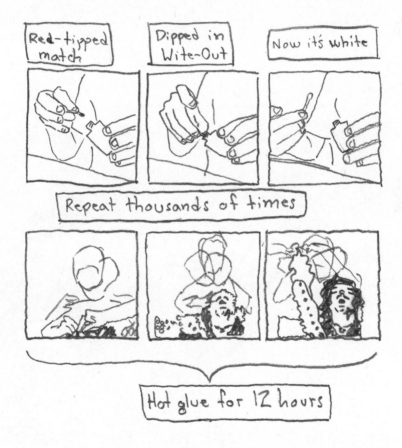

take it so seriously. Therein lay a freedom I'm still trying to comprehend.

After a couple of years, I was making art I previously hadn't been able to imagine. I began to explore other ways outside of pointillism to work with fragments. My experience with the dots made me curious about using words and letters to make a picture. I've always seen single letters as individual elements that can be manipulated. I created images of Martin Luther King Jr. and Malcolm X using words from speeches they'd delivered. I liked both of these approaches, but I was still searching.

It took two years before I'd start experimenting with text again. This time, the approach was to experiment using different pens, pencils, papers, and sizes of letters to write them in a uniform size, but to space them out to create the various shades in the portrait. When I tried this with a black pen, I hit the magic moment. That was the effect I'd been working toward.

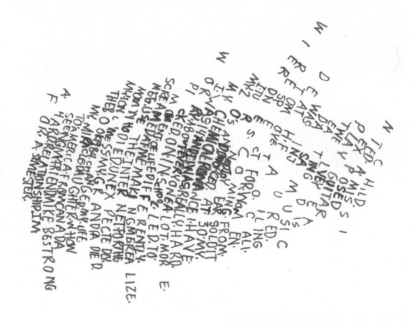

To film, we could not afford to block off busy streets and pay location fees for expensive buildings. So the solution was to go to the empty backstreets and derelict buildings where we didn't have to populate the scene with anything but our key characters. And in order to make that convincing and because the story was hyperbolic, I just simply put the caption "a few years from now" in front of it.

- George Miller

Ultimately, all that experimentation paid off. Back in 2007 after I'd nailed the process, one of these ink-text images became a great success. A major digital news site ran a feature on my work, and the poster sales of that work wound up being enough to pay off my bills and freed me from some financial pressures. I've been doing iterations of this style of text art ever since.

It was startling to realize that all my new art was sparked by a single limitation, which turned out to be the driving force behind a complete transformation of my work. My limitation actually made me a better (and, I guess, a better-known) artist.

Motivated by my neurologist's idea to "embrace the shake," I began to think about all the limitations in my life not as soul-destroying negatives, but rather as a place to concentrate my creativity. Even now that I'm used to working more broadly, with more risks and fewer constraints, I try my hardest to see the barriers in my life as a means to spark my creativity. This may sound a bit masochistic, but now I intentionally go out looking for limitations that I can creatively explore in order to find new ideas. These days, that's a big part of my growth as an artist, and it's become part of what I'm known for. Even the very idea that creativity sucks has grown to serve as a jumping-off point for me. I've thought of all the ways creativity truly sucked, and now I'm systematically exploring them in my art. Seeing our limitations as vehicles for creativity may seem illogical, but it can be just the perspective shift you need in order to open yourself up and transcend your reality.

The next time you feel boxed in, ask yourself these questions:

» What's holding me back?

» What annoys me about this process right now?

Then consider drawing a box, drawing the problem inside, and exploring how this annoying thing could actually help you produce art.

Depending on what barriers you're up against, I get that this idea may seem silly. But what's amazing is that if you can transform one limitation, and then another, and another . . . eventually you will begin to meet all your challenges with far more flexibility. Once you flip that switch in your mind, your limitations will no longer feel like impenetrable roadblocks. Instead, they'll feel more like doorways to new creative paths. Pull that mind trick off, and your work will love you for it. There's no such thing as a limitation. Every obstacle is an opportunity.

7

Honing Your Essence

Our creativity is like this amazing little planet inside all of us. At the center of it is always our core essence. It's that question, that perspective on life, that originally propelled us to pursue our artistic passion in the first place. Mine is that I like to make things. That's it. I know it may seem overly simple, but that's sort of the point. If all my artistic dreams disappeared, if even my skills slipped away, I could still be completely happy as long as I was making things.

My core essence started to develop in high school. I began printing T-shirts. Even then, I had an entrepreneurial streak. I thought maybe I could come up with some funny, edgy designs. I started telling friends about them, and it caught on a little. That experience nudged me toward my next fixation, when I started to come up with funny little cartoons. I found that my friends in art class would give me a laugh, which spurred me to come up with more.

Some were definitely a miss, but after a few months, I had a handful of solid cartoons. What I discovered above everything else was that I enjoyed the process. That experience—just having fun with the work—has remained a central aim for what I do today.

Over time, we slowly accumulate outer layers to our creativity; each one is a ring of influence or a variation on our core essence. On top of it all is our external layer, which is the big career dream we're chasing. A lot of artists spend so much time chasing the big goal in that outer layer that they forget to occasionally look within themselves to see if their core essence still holds true.

If we don't do this regularly, our big goals and our current output can get untethered from our core essence without our even realizing it. We need to be aware of where our creative core is at all times if we want to make art that represents who we are. When we fail to do this, we can lose our way or become disenchanted with our work.

Have you ever created a certain style of art for so long that you think it's hurting your development? Or made art that you know people will like, *but you're already over it?* Or looked at someone else's body of work and compared their style or accomplishments to your own? Feeling dissatisfied with our art often indicates that we've somehow gotten away from our *core creativity* or *creative essence.* Artists who are tuned in to their creative essence feel like their work is exactly where they want it to be. They may still find other people's art fascinating, but they believe in the path they're on.

We stay tuned in to our creative essence by checking in with our passion and spending some time getting our core, our current work, and our big goals aligned again. Remember that everyone's creative heart looks different, and it often changes over time.

Get a TV show about my elaborate pet photography

Be a celebrity pet photographer

Make a pet calendar

Paint pets for friends

Draw pics for friends

Put drawings on shirts

Get graphic design degree

Work at gaming company

Be manager of character design

Open t-shirt business

Expand t-shirt sales online

Make cartoons

Get into school paper

Be a published cartoonist

Outsource design to designers and print shirts overseas

Start a publishing company with a focus on cartoonists

As we grow up, this isn't often what we're guided to think about. Instead, many of us are socialized to focus on the big, flashy, external goals. When we're kids, adults often ask, "What do you want to be when you grow up?"

What do you want to be when you grow up?

When we're kids, the answer is simple . . .	"Artist!"
Then we learn a bit more, and adults ask us to be more specific, so we'll say . . .	"Animator, graphic designer, sculptor, etc."
As many of us leave art college or venture into a creative field, our goals tend to get super specific. We'll say . . .	"Creative director at a small publishing firm, or gallerist in Chelsea in New York, or travel and sell my art in art fairs . . ."

It's entirely possible that one day we will find our current work and our big dreams aren't connecting like they used to. If this happens, we need to take a long look at our entire creative output and honestly ask ourselves, "What is the most basic element of my work that still inspires me?" Try to chip away all the external goals and expectations until you locate what is at the heart of everything that's creative inside you. *This is your core essence.*

Let's say you realize your core desire is to help artists sell their art. In college, you may have dreamed of being a high-powered gallerist in New York City where you sell top-shelf art to elite clientele. That's a fantastic goal, but if you step back, you will actually see that your core essence can be applied in a million different ways.

You could take that core desire and become an artist's manager, or work for a nonprofit that helps artists understand the business side of art, or work for a company that places art in hotels. If you peel back even more layers and examine the depths of your core, you may realize, "Actually, I really just want to help people fulfill their dreams while also helping art get out into the world." Which can be applied to a ton of different careers, in and out of the art world. Our core essences can be really adaptable.

If you ever find yourself feeling disconnected or disenchanted, I suggest you also hit pause and ask yourself, "What do I truly enjoy about my work?" When you get a flicker of a response, dig into that. Sit with it for a while and get familiar with your core purpose again. Do that on a regular basis, and I can guarantee your creativity will stay in line with your heart, which is the creative sweet spot that will intrigue you and keep you fueled for years to come. If you find that your core has changed so much you can't locate it, it's important not to rush the rediscovery process. You don't want to pick up someone else's essence by mistake! And when you do rediscover your essence, really spend some time with it to understand its many nuances, because it can be a slippery sucker to hold on to when life pulls us in so many directions.

8

This one might seem intuitive or old-fashioned. It's called "Work, work, work, work, work!" (And no, Rihanna didn't coin it.) The harder we work toward our goals, the more likely we are to attract creative luck. And when it comes to creativity, hard work is a beautiful thing. And it's important to remember that there's just too much competition these days to expect the gods of luck to show up on your doorstep while you're napping in a hammock.

Trust me: there are few things in life I love more than a lazy weekend. Getting out for a bike ride on a nice day, sitting by the lake, and hanging out with my girlfriend: I live for those moments. But there is something else I love *even more* than that fun stuff—it's making some art over the weekend.

If I see a day with nothing on the calendar, I will wake up, go straight to creating, and try to avoid everything else. Those other things can wait a day or two. Those of us who feel this way may be considered weird by most, but I've found that the more time we give ourselves to get stuff done, the more likely we are to see our creative work develop and find success. Many of us don't punch a clock or answer to a boss when it comes to our creative passion. This means we have to be really disciplined about our work. Staying motivated, even when no one is pushing you (or when you don't feel like working), is an invaluable trait. It can lead you to look back on your career and say, "Wow, I've accumulated a ton of work. How did I do that?" I know how you did it. You worked your tail off!

But working hard is not just about building your résumé. You gotta work to keep your skills sharp. You gotta work to have more success. You gotta work for your own creative development.

I have a friend who worked full-time in grad school while also interning at a demanding company, and she actually requested permission from the chair of the academic department of her university to write an eighty-page thesis. Why such lunacy? Because she was an aspiring author. She knew the deadline for that thesis would force her to learn what it was like to set evenings, weekends, and every second of spare time aside just to write. That's how serious a creative has to be to one day make a living at this stuff.

Here's a bird's-eye view into how it works for me. My average workday isn't thrilling, but it might give you a glimpse into how this work demands you structure your life. I wake up at 6:00 a.m., wander into the kitchen to snag coffee and breakfast, then shower and head to my studio by 7:00 a.m. I use this time to make sure the space is orderly for the day, and I'll try to focus on one thing that interests me—that is, until 9:00 a.m., when the two people I work with come into the studio. At that point, I help them get things rolling. Then I

WORKING HARD IS NOT JUST ABOUT BUILDING YOUR RÉSUMÉ.

usually have a call with a potential client or a call about the details of a job. Then, around 11:00, I head off to lunch.

The afternoon tends to be pretty quiet. I plan things for the next day, set up projects I want to get started on, and check in on what my team is working on. I've learned to expect that I'll get through about 30 percent of what I'd hoped to do—but I've learned that's still a productive day. At that point, I head home and spend time working on smaller projects that fit on the kitchen table. Around 9:00 p.m., I try to shut off the computer and phone. I'll watch a routine TV show to get sleepy and relaxed before I head to bed between 10:00 and 10:30.

It's nothing extraordinary, but maybe it's revealing. I'm not a huge night owl the way some creative people are. I'm a morning person, and I value that quiet time alone in my studio before the team comes in. I also use those early hours judiciously. I cut out the temptation to see what's happening on social media or open my email. If I were to allow those distractions to creep into my mind first thing in the morning, that stuff would spin my head into oblivion and encroach on my prime creating time. My mornings are super focused. That's where I make steady progress on whatever project is in front of me. This sample day also shows how I balance the operation of my business with the more creative side of my work.

I also divide the creative process itself into two distinct categories. I've found that many artists employ this approach so that they always have something to work on, depending on their mood. Some work is mental and some work is physical; so as I like to put it, there's "head work" and there's "hand work." This is often how the creative process plays out because most every art project starts with doing mental work first.

Head Work

Hand Work

Thinking about a new concept you want to explore.

Exploring the new concept with your materials. Possibly running into unforeseen problems.

Thinking about the problems you ran into with the new concept and finding solutions.

Executing those solutions, and getting the project to come together in a way that feels good.

Then things divide, depending on whether you feel like promoting your finished project or reflecting on it for the future.

Promotion

Head Work

Brainstorming ideas to get collectors to see your new work, or how to tweak your new work to increase its viral popularity on social media.

Hand Work

Focusing on all that marketing and PR work that can have a big impact on your income and future projects.

Reflection

Head Work

After some time has passed, you look back at your new project and ask, "What would I do differently? What lessons were learned?"

Hand Work

You make notes and capture all those new ideas so you can go back and apply them in the future.

All artists have both physical and mental work, even if it's not so apparent at first. In order to produce more art and be more efficient with your time, you can do the head work and hand work at different times, depending on your mood, rather than all at once in your work space.

The cool thing about the head work is that creatives can literally do it *anytime, anywhere.* You may feel like thinking about a project when you're commuting to your day job or waiting for an elevator or when you're out with friends and everybody else is taking a couple of minutes to check their phones. For me, traveling for work is a great time to make a list of how to overcome a technical challenge I am up against or brainstorm how I want to promote a project online. Don't wait for your environment to give you permission to create; and conversely, don't waste studio time doing the head work. Think and strategize when you're away from your work space so that the space is as focused as possible on the physical act. Plugging these into other parts of your day makes productive use of your time when you're not in front of the canvas (metaphorically speaking), and it also relieves your mind of all ancillary thoughts so you're free to work.

DON'T WAIT FOR YOUR ENVIRONMENT TO GIVE YOU PERMISSION TO CREATE.

Then, the next time you're creating in your work space, you won't have to build ideas from scratch since you've already done some of the mental heavy lifting outside of your studio.

This way, you don't always have to worry about brainstorming new ideas. You can just focus on the physical side of the project. Doing the mental work at a different time than the physical work can free up a lot of studio time. I remember at my old job as an X-ray tech, I was constantly doing mental work for my art. I carried

> You know, in order to do the DIY punk thing, you have to actually work very, very hard. It's DIY—Do It Yourself. But that takes effort.
>
> — Tom Scharpling

a piece of paper and pencil around with me while I was working so I could capture ideas and write down potential solutions to challenges in current projects that would help me move them forward.

Besides the mental aspect of creation, I would be totally remiss if I didn't emphasize the importance of consistently doing physical creative work. You can't get too far into your own head. Sure, ignoring the physical side momentarily might be okay . . . but over time, it will have a negative impact on a creative person's art in so many ways. The biggest one is that it can cause a fissure between an artist's ideas and their skills, which must work hand in hand at all times.

If we let our ideas get so far ahead of our skills, we'll reach a point where our skills can't actually bring the idea to life. This incredibly frustrating problem has even cut short some art careers. We creatives have to stay physically active with our work because it helps keep our technical skills sharp.

I've also found that artists can make a lot of profound mental discoveries while physically creating. So, don't shut your brain down completely when you're doing physical activities. See what bubbles up. Once you give your brain a challenge, it will subconsciously work on solving it behind the scenes. Let it!

Some artists will have no trouble working their butts off every day. They'll put in a crazy number of hours, seven days a week. But putting in the hard work doesn't automatically mean that our art will transform into what we envisioned. When creating, there are many intangibles that can affect our finished product, so even if we are art machines, we still need to make time in our day to step back and look at the bigger picture. Sometimes, it's hard to know when to say "This project is done," so we work on it way beyond its natural point of completion. It's never easy to shake up our creative process, but it's important to stay aware of how it has worked in the past compared to how it's working now.

For me, there are days when I feel like doing nothing but mental work, like brainstorming new ideas or reconceptualizing old ones. When I'm experiencing a nice flow of ideas, I'll ride that wave as long as I can and allow myself to focus entirely on ideation. Then, on days when I'm struggling with the more intellectual side of my art, I don't push it. I just switch gears and work on something physical for a bit. There's a certain mindfulness practice in that physical work that often clears the mind for "head work"–type solutions to fall into place when you don't expect it.

Everyone has a different creative process. If you can monitor your internal creative ebb and flow and give yourself permission to work on whatever fits your mood, this process can be incredibly useful to your creative production.

9

Have I made my point yet? Let's hit it hard here: your creative life will not exist if you do not give it adequate time.

When I landed my first real job after graduating college, I was really excited. I finally had some money—think of all the art supplies I could buy! But then I realized all the free time I'd so effortlessly set aside for my art for years suddenly disappeared. Juggling a full-time job and a burgeoning art career was going to involve some trade-offs.

Before long, I felt like one of the faceless cogs in the machine. Each day I went into a job and worked all day, then went home to relax, sleep, rinse, and repeat. And I was meant to (gulp) do this for the rest of my life? Ugh. I was struggling to find time to create. I didn't figure it out as quickly as I could have, but through many attempts and failures, I discovered how I could function creatively with a full-time job: I had to intentionally, and with great effort and social sacrifice, make time for my art. *We all do.*

Lots of super-famous creatives had day jobs at one time: T. S. Eliot was a banker, Mark Rothko was a teacher, Philip Glass was a taxi driver *and* a plumber. Ask any artist with a long career and they'll tell you they had to make a deliberate effort to keep creating through all their commitments and the changes life threw their way. You don't accidentally have free time and spend it working on a project; we artists have to plan our days with discipline kicked up a notch . . . and since organization is not a natural strength for many artists, this can be a huge challenge.

If you're a young artist with no family obligations or kids, you may assume that free time falls from the sky. But when you get older, you'll find it all seems to evaporate, whether into a sea of work responsibilities or parental duties. So, what does an artist with a busy life do? Again: we make time. A while back, I met a musician who I admired. She told me her goal every weekend was to "have nothing to do." She did this because all that unclaimed "free time" could go toward her music. *What a power move,* I thought. Could I do the same thing?

It doesn't matter if you're married or single, it's a lofty goal to clear every single weekend for your art. For most of us to get to that point, we'd have to change how we behave, how we socialize, and how we date, work, shop, live, and act as consumers. Can you see the challenge? You kinda have to rearrange your entire life for your art.

So, let's get organized. Have you ever charted how you spend your time? It can be eye-opening. How about doing it now? In the space here, mark when you wake up and go to sleep. Then slowly fill in your day with all the daily activities that you can't change—

My day

5am

6

7

8

9

10

11

12pm

1

2

3

4

5

6

7

8

9

10

11

12am

1

like going to work, school, commuting, unloading the dish-washer . . . the real-life daily stuff.

As you go through your day, note where you might find some free time. It will take some sacrifice and (yes) some creativity to do this. You may even find that you have to decide between a favorite show and creating, but maybe you can do both.

Copy this chart a few times if you'd like to examine your routine over the course of a week.

Now that you see your daily routine laid out in all its jam-packed glory, here are three ways you can create some extra free time in your life:

» **Literally Free Up Some Time.** Start massaging your calendar. Try taking a Saturday activity (laundry? Target run?) and moving it to Monday evening. Did you find any free time? Here's another: try not to make any plans on Friday nights. Clean the house so Saturday's wide open, or get to bed early to wake up and spend the weekend working. Or can you move some of your shopping online and skip the trip to the store? And what about your internet habits? Are you losing your evenings to time-sucking websites and social media? Step away from them! Look for those time savers. I guarantee you can free up some time if you seriously set that intention.

» **Adapt Your Work to Your Limitations.** See if you can break up your projects into manageable, bite-size chunks. If you can work on some components independently, you may free up time and discover a new technique you wouldn't have tried before. Back when I was an X-ray tech, one aspect of my job was to sit around and wait for patients. So, I turned that into my creative brainstorming and problem-solving art time.

» **Shift the Kind of Work You Create.** No one wants to settle for smaller goals, but maybe shifting today's goals slightly is what keeps your dream real for tomorrow. Imagine you're a filmmaker, but your day job doesn't give you the time to make full-length films. Why not work on a short film? It

YOUR COMMITMENT TO YOUR CREATIVITY IS YOUR COMMITMENT TO YOURSELF.

could get you some exposure and connections that could help make your big dream of shooting features a reality in the next couple of years.

The bottom line? Your commitment to your creativity is your commitment to yourself. Be willing to rearrange your schedule and reprioritize your life so that you're never abandoning your greatest love by putting your creativity on the shelf.

10

Creativity Is Hard on Relationships

Yes, our work takes time and commitment, and there's another factor in this mix that might also produce some questions. If you happen to be a creative person who falls in love with that one special soul who totally gets you and your work, then congratulations. You've won the lottery.

But even with the most supportive and tolerant partner, one night you might wake up in a cold sweat and realize: *Wait, my creative projects take passion, energy, and time . . . and this relationship takes passion, energy, and time.* You only have so much of all three, right? Something's got to give. This is a universal fear among artists: how do you prioritize your love for another person with your love of creating?

Most people have this wild idea that when the workday is through, couples should be available to hang out together, talk about their day, grab a bite to eat, or just Netflix and chill. Of course, many artists think differently about that because (hello) most of us are not normal . . . at all!

That's why so many creative people spend their lives walking a tightrope between managing creative time and relationship time. When you're in a relationship, time spent on projects can be easily interpreted as time not spent with your significant other—so there is this constant push and pull between the two loves. One big rub is that if you're living a creative life and you have a day job, then the only time you can create is when you get home . . . which bumps into your relationship time. This can cause all sorts of problems with your significant other.

HOW DO YOU PRIORITIZE YOUR LOVE FOR ANOTHER PERSON WITH YOUR LOVE OF CREATING?

Not only that, but when creative people do have free time, many will eagerly choose to stay in and work rather than hang out with friends or family, see a show, or have dinner out with another couple. We're not trying to be annoying, but our tendency to take our work super seriously can occasionally be a turn-off to the people we care about—especially our partner.

It's about sharing priorities, or clearly and consistently respecting each other's priorities. If a creative person wants to show their love to their partner by treating them to a romantic date, you should know it may not be a typical date-night dinner. It might be a quirky, inexpensive meal somewhere off the beaten path. We would rather drive a clunky car, skip splurging on furniture from an upscale home-furnishing chain, or forgo luxury hotels for all eternity in order to have more attention and money to spend on our creative projects. Creative types often find the most beauty in everyday life, and we need partners who are similar or who aspire to live a simpler life. That's why we need to stay aware of how our differing priorities affect our relationship, and do our best to listen to our partner's needs.

When we have creative passions but our partner does not, we have to find a way to balance our days so we're including our partner in our waking life on a regular basis. (Sleeping next to each other doesn't count.)

From my experience, if you can't find a working balance between your partner and your creative work, one of these situations may occur:

» You'll devote all your time to your creative work, and then suddenly wake up one day and realize your relationship is on the rocks.

» You will push your creative work aside to spend time with your partner so often that one day, you realize all the creativity has been squeezed out of your life. Then you'll be unhappy, which is a disaster on both fronts.

Life has shown me that communication is often the missing piece to any happy relationship. It's not always easy, but talking it out is the best way to get two people on the same page, or at least give them a better understanding of where the other person is coming from, even if they don't necessarily agree. There are times in my relationship when one of us feels like everything is good, but the other feels lonely. So, communicate with that person you love! Let them know that you have a different set of priorities than the average person. Tell them you love spending time with them, but you need to create to feel like yourself. My hope for you is that they'll at least try to understand.

If you are a creative person dating another creative person, then you get the fun of balancing both of your creative lives. One universal tip is to let that person have their space, too. If your significant other is working on their project while you're free, then prepare to hang out alone sometimes or schedule that time with friends. If you've both been spending tons of time on projects,

TALKING IT OUT IS THE BEST WAY TO GET TWO PEOPLE ON THE SAME PAGE.

make a concerted effort to hit pause and find some time to be together in your waking hours. Having projects to work on is awesome, but having your projects and someone to love is even better. We all need love in our lives. Even us creative hermits.

Committed relationships can be really tough on a person's creativity, but they can also be amazingly inspiring and nourishing to your art and your soul. If you can work together to establish this balance and flow, not only will you create lots of cool work; you'll also have someone to love and share your life with, which can actually be an important component to a happy and fulfilled art career.

11

Creative Buddy

There's one kind of relationship that can really bolster your art, and this is a tip that has helped my career a lot. Having a creative buddy—someone in your life who will be your sounding board when you're considering what to work on and how—can be a massive catapult to your creative career.

Over the years I've had many creative buddies. But not long ago, I had a great one. This person was the perfect creative sound-board for me because they were genuinely curious about life in general, as well as my art career. They would dig, prod, question, wonder aloud, and never judge me for my wildest ideas. They also gave me one of the most useful pieces of advice. I remember kicking around the idea of creating a picture of Nikola Tesla with electric shocks, and figuring out how to make it happen seemed easy on one hand, but also was technically hard. All electric shocks

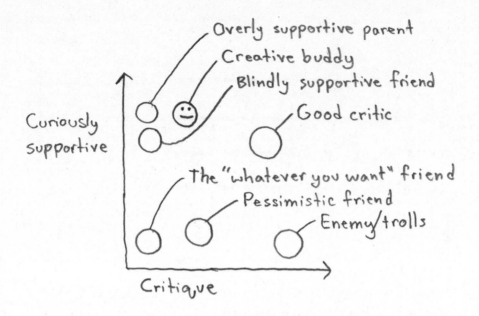

Overly supportive parent
Creative buddy
Blindly supportive friend
Good critic
Curiously supportive
The "whatever you want" friend
Pessimistic friend
Enemy/trolls
Critique

aren't equal. "It's just expertise. Go get help," my creative buddy said. That push was all I needed, and that project turned out to be one of my favorites. (Over the years, it also landed the top spot on Reddit and Imgur.)

But I might not have pursued hunting down expertise if my creative buddy hadn't given me the nudge I needed. Art is personal and illogical, and sharing thoughts and questions with someone is really important.

Some artists can create masterworks from hermetically sealed caves and find success working solo. But it's important for us to have a buddy we can share new ideas with—someone who's down to dialogue with you. We all need that person who listens. A killer creative buddy is someone who cares about your art, is totally supportive, and will give you just the right type of nudge when you're

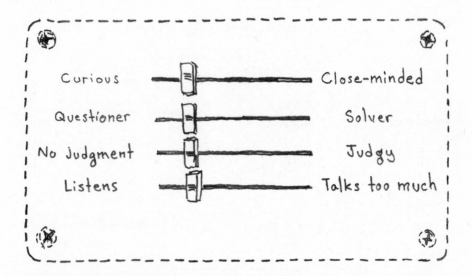

Curious ——————|——————— Close-minded

Questioner ——————|——————— Solver

No Judgment ——————|——————— Judgy

Listens ——————|——————— Talks too much

off track, scared, or lazy. If your creative buddy sounds like the perfect friend, that's because they *kinda are*.

One day, while I happened to be missing the bond I'd shared with my buddy, I was leading a small-group discussion at an event for a big company. For the event, the corporation gathered a group of their most creative employees tasked with developing the next "big thing" for their company. My role was to move around and spark creative conversations, and I was curious how many of them had a creative buddy. Want to know what I found?

Every creative person wants that perfect creative confidante, but finding a creative buddy has never been more challenging. How is that possible? Well, have you tried getting someone on the phone lately? How many people do you know who will eagerly line up to have a meandering conversation about your work at 2:00 p.m., let alone at 2:00 a.m.? I'm available, but I think I may be in the minority.

If you're looking for a creative buddy, don't pick the person trying to solve your question or problem quickly. The role of a creative

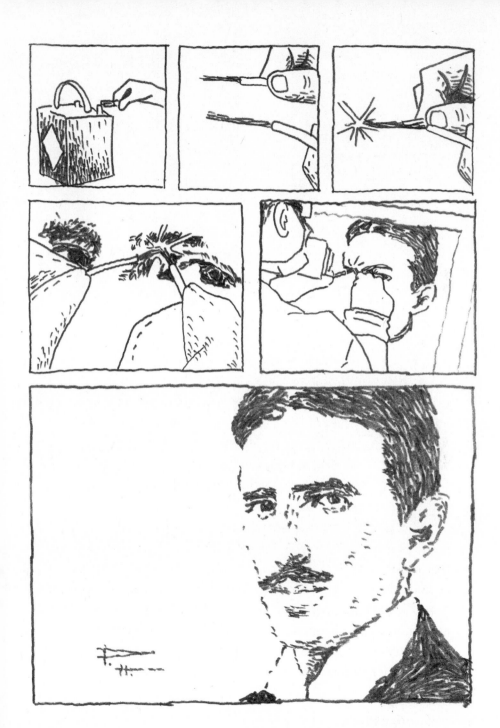

Only 20% of the creatives in the room had a creative buddy. That's it.

Around 25% had someone they liked to share ideas with, but their buddy would often shut down their ideas prematurely.

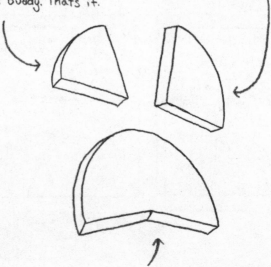

55% of the creatives in the room had nobody to share their ideas with. And they were really curious how I could help them get one.

buddy is just the opposite. They take their time, they're engaged, they ask questions, and they listen. That's the key. The right creative buddy's goal is not to "fix" things for you, because there's no single answer to a creative problem or quest; their goal is to nudge you down the path.

Give your search plenty of time, because the impact of meeting the right supporter at any given moment could last your whole lifetime. I've found it's also likely that you can have many creative buddies throughout the course of your career.

Here's one way to feel out whether you've found your creative buddy. Number one: do they do a decent job listening to you blab? Hey—that's a great start. Maybe mention that you would like to share some ideas with them . . . then watch how they respond. Did

-Wanted-
Someone to chat about cool projects we are both working on
Desires: open conversation
Listen, stoke, ask questions
Tell me about your project and I'll tell you about mine
mynameis7445 @gmail.com
mynameis7445 @Gmail.com
mynameis7445 @gmail.com
mynameis7445 @Gmail.com
mynameis7445 @gmail.com

they ask good questions and offer valuable suggestions? Does it feel like you're ready to move forward with an idea after talking to them? If you answered yes, then you may have found the right one.

But you may also explore this kind of relationship with several people only to find you don't quite click. That's okay, too. Just like any great relationship in life, cre-ative buddies can be rare. And when you find your creative buddy? Take great care of them. Don't take them

YOU HAVE TO BE A GOOD BUDDY TO HAVE A GOOD BUDDY.

for granted, will ya? Show your gratitude on the regular and treat your buddy like they're valued. And remember that you have to be a good buddy to have a good buddy. Giving our time, thought, and attention to others is a great way to make discoveries about what we're looking for in our own lives. It's also a joy to see other people noodle their way through an idea.

12

There Are
No Rules

We've got to follow rules in life, but when it comes to creativity, it's empowering to cut the red tape and do what you want. When you learn how to tell the difference between rules and expectations or societal pressures, you'll notice how the flow, volume, and sheer quality of your art will start to thrive.

In childhood, we're inundated with rules because they help us little monsters prepare to live in the world on our own one day. Following rules works for kids, but in the creative world, it can be a pretty limiting practice. Breaking—or at least bending—the rules is a much more powerful tactic for an artist. But many of us learn social norms and expectations that we unintentionally take on as our own beliefs.

Have you ever thought about how following rules affects your creativity?

I recently read about a study that found people who have rigid

> I didn't care about what people thought of me and I didn't care what I thought of myself, so I would go to the far reaches of my dark side and pull these horrors out of my soul and put them on the catwalk.
>
> - Alexander McQueen

belief systems tend to be less mentally flexible. (In other words, less creative.)

Why is that? It's because having a rigid belief system means you'll have a hard time seeing things outside of their classic categories. Take two friends who have cereal, milk, and spoons but don't have a bowl. One shrugs and grimaces, resigned that there's simply no vessel from which to procure each spoonful. But the other asks: "What if we pour milk into the cereal bag?" That's prime execution. This is how a strict adherence to so-called rules can limit our thinking and results.

We've been so conditioned to follow rules that we don't even notice that we operate by them anymore. Let's break it down: when it comes to art, there are no rules.

I went out and I got an agent. I lied, I created a whole résumé that was fake.

- Josh Brolin

I meet students all the time who confess they've allowed rules to govern their vision of what's possible in their careers. You need a bachelor's degree to get a job in the arts, and you need a master of fine arts degree to show in a gallery. Huh? No, you don't. Who knows where these things get started, but I'm here to tell you that they're not always true. Are they indicators that speak to a trend? Maybe. I get that some art-related jobs (like working at a museum) require certain degrees to apply. Even so, most art students still talk like the degree is *the thing*—when it's really your skill that gets you the gig every time.

EXPRESSION DELIGHTS IN FREEDOM, AND RULES OFTEN STIFLE EXPRESSION.

Almost every rule you ever heard about how to live a creative life can be smashed to bits. All artists break rules, especially the icons. It isn't entirely about rebellion—it's more about freedom of expression. Expression delights in freedom, and rules often stifle expression.

Stay focused on learning the tools and techniques you need to master your craft. Gather as much knowledge as you can, but when rules become barriers? Push them aside. Crush them. Hulk out on that shit. The process is completely yours.

Think about it this way: break a law, and you may go to jail. Stretch a norm, and people may say you're weird. Use your creativity to break an art rule? Do that, and you're freaking brilliant.

1

Idea Filter

An idea is born. When we're kids, we all have this wonderful ability to form ideas and then instantly channel them out into the world through speech. But as we get older, we realize our free-flowing idea funnel can get us into trouble sometimes. We begin running our ideas through an internal gauntlet of cagey critics that I call our "idea filter," which can be an amazing sorting tool when functioning properly. Unfortunately, it can also sabotage your idea flow if you don't keep it calibrated.

If you feel like you're being way too hard on your ideas, it may be a good time to get under the hood of your filter to make sure it's working for you and not against you. Our filters are predominantly composed of our personal tastes, our life experiences, and what we learn in school—but our filters are not totally insular. They're also heavily influenced by external factors, like the environment

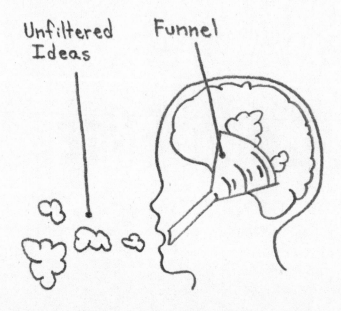

Unfiltered Ideas

Funnel

we're creating in, the audience we're creating for, and our motivation for working on a creative project in the first place.

Let's say you're in your elementary school art class. You're having a lot of fun exploring your creativity. Ideas are flowing seamlessly out of your mental funnel. Life is great. Then one day, your friend Billy tells you that one of your ideas is the dumbest thing he's ever heard. Just like that, your funnel becomes a filter. Suddenly, there's a layer in your filter that is rejecting all the ideas you think Billy might find dumb in future art classes. But then you go home, where there is no Billy, and his layer instantly disappears—so your filter becomes a funnel again, and everything runs smoothly. (In your face, Billy!)

Except the next day, your supportive mom (sigh—of all people) casually mentions that your new work is "a little juvenile for some-

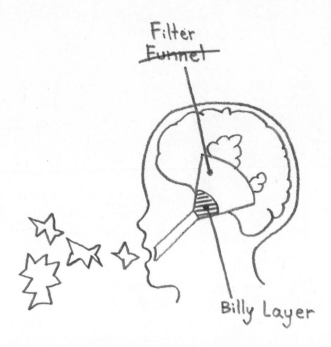

Filter ~~Funnel~~

Billy Layer

one your age." Whaaat? *Et tu*, Mama? Now your idea filter has a Billy layer *and* an overbearing Mom layer. Watching this develop, you see your childhood playfulness and your free-flowing funnel ride off into the sunset to go have their own fun . . .

Are you beginning to see how these personal layers can add up? Repeat this process throughout your life and your filter might accumulate countless layers for girlfriends/boyfriends, teachers, parents, coworkers, bosses, frenemies, art heroes, *and of course, Billy*. With your idea filter chock-full of layers, you may notice that only a trickle of fresh ideas are even making the cut anymore. That's when you have to ask yourself, "Is my filter trying to please everyone else in my life?" You may come up with tons of new ideas each day, but if your filter is spiking them all before you have a

chance to act . . . then is your idea filter really serving your creative interests?

When it's functioning well, a filter can be an amazing tool for creative output. I wouldn't recommend anyone disable theirs entirely. Your filter is what helps you choose which projects to work on and lets you develop a personal style. It also helps you focus on one specific aspect of your creativity so you don't get lost in a cloud of ideas. Your filter can make your work great! But it can also get so clogged that it's amazing when anything makes it out at all. This is one of the reasons creative block can hit.

Depending on my mood or what I'm working on, my filter may be set to "free-flowing art libertine," or if I'm feeling a little down, it may involuntarily be set to "fetal position neurotic guy." That is one fantastic upside to our idea filters: no one is stuck with a de-

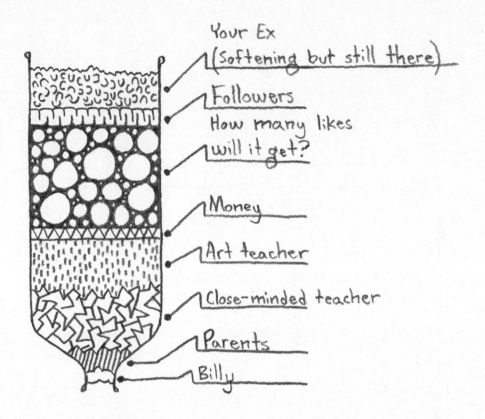

Your Ex
(Softening but still there)

Followers
How many likes
will it get?

Money

Art teacher

Close-minded teacher

Parents

Billy

fective filter for life. They're very adaptable tools that can be constantly recalibrated, tweaked, and adjusted. You can tinker with yours so much that, eventually, you'll know exactly how it's going to affect your idea flow and how to recalibrate it—so it's always producing good ideas

NO ONE IS STUCK WITH A DEFECTIVE FILTER FOR LIFE.

and not screwing with your head. If you really believe that all your ideas are total rubbish, there's a good possibility that you're putting too much pressure on yourself.

INSTRUCTIONS

Think of a place you create in or people you create for. Label it and create all the filter layers that your mind considers when creating. I started you out by labeling the first one.

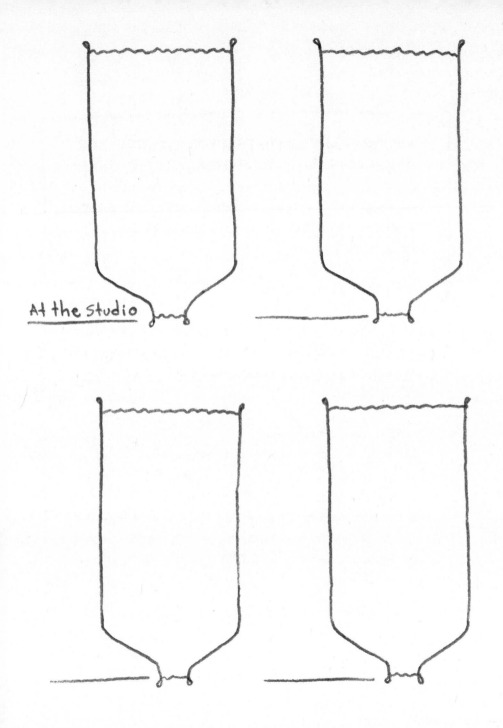

At the studio

ARE THERE ANY LAYERS THAT YOU CAN ADJUST OR REMOVE TO LET YOUR CREATIVITY FLOW?

Now if you want to dive deep into your own psyche to better understand where your filter is coming from, try asking yourself these three questions:

1. Who Are You Creating For?
Is a specific person in your creative orbit affecting your filter? (Interesting, right?) Who do you let influence your new ideas? Why do you let them have a say in your creativity? What pressures are you putting on yourself because of the people around you? Be honest!

2. Where Are You Creating It?
Now, imagine a situation where you are filtering a ton of creative ideas. Look around: where are you? Is it a conservative environment, or one where you can think freely? It might be fun to spontaneously create with a friend at home, but you might be hesitant to do it in a class with thirty people staring at you. Ask yourself, "Is it possible that my filter is being affected by my environment?"

3. Why Are You Creating in the First Place?

Is the "why" of it all adding unnecessary grit to your filter? Ask yourself, "Am I doing this project for me or for someone else? Am I doing it out of desire or out of necessity?" Once you answer those questions, ask yourself whether the reason you're pursuing this creative idea is actually causing your filter to run more slowly. Let's say you're writing a novel that you hope will be turned into a movie. Knowing that your work could one day be produced by a major studio can put some extra pressure on your writing. The same thing goes for everyone in any creative field. Making something for fun, making something to sell, or making something to achieve some level of fame will put unnecessary pressure on your creativity.

I've found that most artists, no matter how good we are, really need to work to keep our ideas flowing through the years, even if that means tricking the critical part of our brains every once in a while so it will let us play around in our work without worrying about failure. So, get to know your filter. One day soon, those so-called crappy ideas your filter's been shredding on sight will suddenly be viewed as potential little gems to be nurtured and loved.

2

Don't let praise fuel you or hate cool you

When you've reached the stage in which you know who you are as an artist, identifying your essence has helped keep your idea filter clean and wide open, and generating fresh projects is coming so naturally that you're starting to build a little audience—congratulations! You've just achieved a new level of vulnerability that comes with opening your work to criticism.

(Isn't creativity fun?)

When my art gets slammed or praised by the outside world, I try to let both experiences slide past me equally like I was practicing some form of creative tai chi. Of course I'm not always successful in these attempts. But I've found it saves me a lot of sleepless nights to focus on the next project and to not get caught up in the hype or hate. Did I magically stop caring how people respond to my art? Oh, I still care . . . a lot. But I've learned that my desire to be a popular artist is not nearly as strong as my desire to make art that connects with who I am.

For instance, I've found people generally respond best to my playful pop art, like a portrait I once made of Kurt Cobain. In that piece, I smashed an electric guitar, then arranged the broken pieces into an image of Kurt's grungy visage, which I also eventually destroyed. If I chased the praise I got from this piece, I'd probably still be making artwork like this.

I know that because I tried doing it a few years ago. While my work during that period received a lot of attention, I eventually found myself creating art that I didn't genuinely care about. It took some time, but I worked my way back to making art that connects with my core. I told myself: *I will not let praise fuel me or hate cool me. I'm in charge of my own creativity.* If we become positive feedback magnets, then soon, we won't be creating for ourselves. We will be creating for our fans in an attempt to get more of that intoxicating feedback, which is when praise can become really dangerous.

IF WE BECOME POSITIVE FEEDBACK MAGNETS, THEN SOON, WE WON'T BE CREATING FOR OURSELVES.

That's why I feel it's so important for us artists to never stop building up our own creative self-worth. Your confidence can function like a force field that keeps you safely producing art, your way. The confidence you have in your artistic direction is like a bubble that you can create, free of influence. Good or bad.

One tip for defanging haters is to cut the emotional cord on

your projects—fast. Whenever you finish a new work and release it into the wild, untether your feelings from your baby ASAP. A pony learns to walk an hour after it's born. The minute you finish a piece, trust that it will be able to survive without you. You can't allow negative reviews to stop you from creating, and you've got to get off that dizzying emotional ride before it kills your confidence and creativity. If you let praise take you on a high, then you're also giving a horrible review the power to send you plummeting. And the simple reality is, we never know how our work will be received when we show it off.

Case in point: a few years ago, I had an idea to create this odd little maze book. A publisher said they loved the spirit of it, and they wondered whether I was interested in taking it beyond mazes to develop a book of artistic activities that inspired kids to explore their creativity. When it was published, it got some nice reviews, and the publisher let me know they were going to promote it on their social media page, which got me pretty excited. *Look out, bestseller list!* I thought. But take a look at the "promo" they posted on Facebook to sell my book:

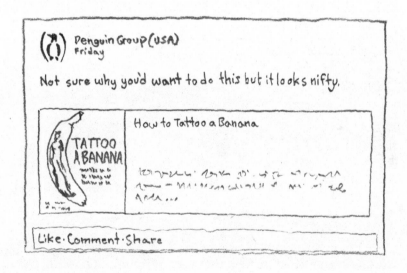

It wasn't exactly what I'd anticipated. But practicing my creative tai chi to counteract the sting of rejection was pretty easy when I really thought about it. I knew that the person in charge of their Facebook account was probably an intern who never read the

One of the vulnerabilities of being visible is that when you are visible you can be seen, and when you can be seen you can be touched and when you can be touched you can be hurt. So all of us have these elaborate ways of looking as if we are showing up and not showing up.

- David Whyte

book (and maybe had no idea that part of their responsibility was to completely champion the publisher's list of titles). Regardless of what anyone thought, I believed my book was nifty. So, I laughed and said, "Welp, guess you can't win them all!"

I've had people mock the supplies I use and slam me for wasting food on my work. I've lost connections with people who I planned to work with on a piece that I wound up walking away from because it had been too much for me to take on. Over the years, yeah, at times, you let people down. You stretch yourself too thin. You set out with the most optimistic vision and committed intention for every project, and sometimes it just doesn't work out. And because so much of your work, even when it's unfinished, is subject to an audience's opinion, there are times when you piss people off. It sucks.

Not letting hate or praise affect your art is a tricky maneuver . . . but in principle, it's actually simple to achieve. Here's something that helps: when I'm developing any project, I no longer make promises I can't keep. I might ask people to be involved in certain projects, but I make no pledge that I will post the finished work. I don't want people to feel like I owe them anything. I've also learned that I don't like being paid for the projects that I want to do for *me*. Then I feel like I'm working for someone.

And when a work goes live, I have to separate the part of my personality that is influenced by the outside world from the side of my personality that's not influenced by anyone. Once I have them isolated, I give them separate jobs. I let my externally influenced side handle my PR and marketing, while I keep the "totally me" side of my personality insulated from the outside world so it's free to run my idea creation. It took practice, but now it's somewhat natural and can really work.

3

Crush Your Idols

When it comes to comparing our jobs, our appearances, or our lives with other people's, our culture doesn't do the most solid job of reminding us not to have too much envy in our hearts (or our social feeds). Everywhere you look, there's somebody who appears to be better than you in a multitude of ways. It's also intense in the creative world, where you rarely hear anyone tell you to "beware of idol worship." This is unfortunate, because the danger of putting your heroes on a pedestal is real for a lot of artists.

Initially, it can be motivating to hold the pros you admire in high esteem. They give you something to aim for, which inspires you to reach for lofty heights. The problem is that this also causes some artists to lose motivation and go into that "I'll never be that good; I guess that's not the life for me" mode. In turn, they may stop trying so hard. It's normal to have moments of doubt, but it's not the best reason to stop. There's always going to be somebody more skilled, more famous, more successful. Your idols know that and feel the same way sometimes. For real.

A lot of artists live secretive lives shrouded in mystique, but if the people who inspire you the most have an early career you can track, you'll probably discover the unexpected. Look deeper into the early work or lives of most famous artists, and you'll often discover a struggling misfit who started from the exact same point you did. **OUR HEROES ARE REAL PEOPLE.** He or she was working just as hard as you are to make it, and they looked up to their own heroes. We all have them, no matter how far up the food chain an artist ultimately goes.

The challenge for us as individuals is to figure out how to use these examples so they are helping, and not hurting, our creative flow. One tip I live by these days is that I don't put any person on some unreachable pedestal. Picture them on something more accessible, like a hill. It's a lot less daunting to climb a hill than it is to scale a cliff.

Another important point of reflection is to think: what exactly do I admire about this person? Look past their art and identify those characteristics. Often you'll find that you identify something within them that *you already hold inside yourself.* This suggests that you don't have to become somebody else. You just have to continue working so those elements rise up from your work.

And remember that our heroes are real people. They have a lot more happening in their lives besides their art and a lot more going on than we can see. They have relationships, personalities, weekend get-togethers, dishes in the sink, and all sorts of things. When they're not busy doing a great job of sharing their work with those around them, they're just like you and me. Don't strive for their fame, fortune, or persona. Strive to be you. It's passion, discipline, and work ethic that will one day bring you to where they are today. The only aspect that you should try to replicate is another artist's explorative nature. That's the risk that comes with real rewards.

The next time you fall for that new super-hot artist, don't ask yourself, "Why can't I be them?" Instead look at aspects of their life that clearly bring them authentic happiness. Let that be one of the gauges on your dashboard for creative success.

4

The Burden of Immortality

A story:

When Sam was a kid, she created for fun and would eventually lose track of what she made. In high school, she put a picture in a frame for the first time and felt a sense of accomplishment and pride. Years later, she came back from college and saw that old drawing. It made her cringe a little. She wanted to replace it with something better. Somewhere in this time frame, she had the idea that she should only be creating things that will stand the test of time. Slowly this notion began to block every creative idea she had. She felt paralyzed. She stopped practicing art.

The end.

I just shuddered thinking about that predicament. It's weird how you can begin to pressure your creativity to behave in a way it's not designed to. Creativity is about now, about this moment. Don't put undue pressure on your creativity in your attempt to be a revered artistic figure for the next thousand years. It's natural to have goals for your work, whether your aim is to sell art to the public, construct a gift for a friend, or create art for some commercial audience. It seems logical that artists should want to shape their work, considering it will live on for the whole of eternity . . . right?

It depends on who you ask. In my mind, there are two sides of the spectrum.

This is a tricky dance, and I feel like we should always lean toward letting the creativity flow unhindered. When you think of

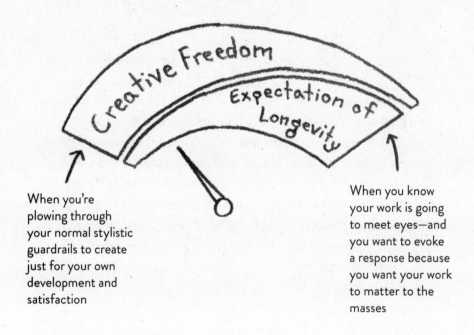

When you're plowing through your normal stylistic guardrails to create just for your own development and satisfaction

When you know your work is going to meet eyes—and you want to evoke a response because you want your work to matter to the masses

some of the most renowned artists throughout time, their eternal fame seems to come from the fact that they created whatever they fancied.

I've met tons of artists who claim they're only creating art for their own enjoyment—but when I get them talking about their projects in depth, they often let it slip that they wanted to impress other people. This can be a clue that they have a blind spot. I know I've had plenty.

Sometimes even today, I'll hit pause on a project and wonder: *Is this the art I want to be making now, or have I subconsciously tweaked this concept so other people would like it more?* If I'm honest with myself, sometimes I'll have to admit that yeah, I've been adjusting my concept so it will appeal to others. This realization can be painful for any artist who thinks they're totally independent, but I've found that very few creative thinkers can avoid working with zero degree of influence from the outside world. Even famed artists from the past who seemed to make whatever they desired were probably driven by forces around them to some degree.

CREATIVITY IS ABOUT NOW, ABOUT THIS MOMENT.

Of course, there are times when we don't care what other people think at all. We may be working outside our usual zone, because it really and truly has no set audience other than us. So, knowing that, don't toss out the next super-subversive idea you have just because you think you're the only audience for it. If you're worried it's so weird that it could hurt your professional reputation, you could always try creating an alter ego on social media that could be a safe place for you to share all your risky art pieces. I will never actually admit that I've done this before, but let's just say: *I definitely recommend it.*

Our projects can have a life we never imagined. Maybe your hope is for people to be so into your work that they buy it. When that's the case, what do you do? A lot of us make more! Hopefully that sells, too, and then people start to collect it because your name is getting out there. And one day long from now, after you're gone, your work will be bought up over time by museums and wealthy collectors. It could be considered invaluable, so it's made part of the permanent collection at the Louvre. Or maybe you'll make something and someone will buy it; but then when they pass away, their grandkids donate it to Goodwill. Maybe it's worth five bucks, or maybe it will be talked about on the news because somebody bought it for five bucks but was able to sell it for two hundred thousand. That cosmic algorithm that bestows value on art is part of what makes this work so tingly.

DO WORK THAT MATTERS TO YOU TODAY.

The most important thing is to entertain yourself first. Try not to get hung up on what might come of your work down the road. Do work that matters to you today. I come up with tons of ideas, and my greatest hope is that one of them will effectively hook my own attention. If not, I consider which would be the hardest to create or the coolest to see come together. That's the one I go for next.

Your endgame should not be eternal fame or even a momentary reaction from a stranger. I don't worry about what happens to a piece of work after I've completed it. Time spent speculating is time not spent creating something more.

5

The Surprise Benefits of the Shiny Ball

It starts when we're kids goofing around at the playground, at an amusement park, or on a device. Surrounded by so much entertainment, we can't resist trying everything, always enchanted by the next shiny ball in our path.

No matter our age, we humans love to have a buffet of choices. Even after you're grown up, shiny ball syndrome can be a powerful distraction in your life. In your creative mode, this means getting so excited about the next project or pursuing the next hot idea that you're leaving a bunch of half-finished projects behind you.

Those experiencing shiny ball syndrome are often in the early stages of their careers and always gravitating to what attracts them in the moment. They never really commit themselves to any one idea.

You might chase the shiny ball because . . .

» It can be a great way to learn a new skill. If the reason to start a new project is to gain a new skill, toss those partially finished projects in the trash and learn!

» You're discovering your personal style. Developing a style is one of the hardest things to do. Staying in the process and not finishing things in order to discover what makes your art unique is a great way to find yourself as an artist rather than focusing on getting a completed picture to hang on the wall.

» You want to stay energized. Completing projects can take a lot of energy. Keeping your enthusiasm up by starting something new and then carrying that energy over to another ongoing project is an awesome way to control your motivation.

» You love the process of inspiration, discovery, and development . . . and wrapping up a project is rarely as interesting. (This sounds like me! Totally understand.)

» It helps you move on from a tough project. Sometimes it feels better to start something new and focus on the sense of possibility that it offers than feel crushed when a big project doesn't go the way you planned.

Can anyone really say if following the shiny ball is good or bad? This depends. I've met a lot of working artists who were born to jump around, so they bounce all over their work space with ten projects going at once. They've told me they love not feeling pressure to constantly crank out finished art, which is a perfectly fine method for creating.

If this sounds like you, I'd like you to think about what part of the creative process you enjoy most . . . then just milk it. It's a rare gift to be a maker who gets to create for the sheer joy of it. If you're not on a deadline to satisfy a client and not under the gun to make a sale, then go after the shiny ball all you like.

But if you're someone who relies on your art to make a living, then you've gotta get 'er done. Following the shiny ball can be a career killer if you have to produce art on a daily basis for deadlines or clients. Although it's not impossible, selling a half-finished work of art can be very challenging. But if this is who you are, heck, why not sell your half-finished projects as completed works of art? No one ever said artwork has to be fully realized. You could even sell your half-finished works as political statements on the collective attention-deficit disorder that's overtaken our modern society. Remember? There are no rules!

For the shiny ball types who'd like to rein it in and get disciplined, make a pledge to yourself not to start anything new until you've finished your present project . . . even if it's not going to plan.

On the spectrum of shiny ballers (that's a thing, right?), I like to think I zigzag between income and joy. I will produce one project for work, then I'll indulge in a fun project that is totally for me. But sometimes, even now, I'll beat myself up because I've fallen for the shiny ball again and moved on to another project too quickly. Before I start the public lashings, I always stop and ask myself: *Am I really distracted by a shiny ball, or am I moving on from that project on purpose?*

There are times when a shiny ball takes you away from a bad

project, proving something important: that you trust your instincts. If your gut tells you that a project isn't going to work for whatever reason and you just cannot get

TRUST YOUR INSTINCTS. motivated to continue working on it, this could be one of those instances when it's smart to just move on. Life is too short to toil away for weeks or months on something that bores you, fills you with dread, or makes you feel a little dead inside.

There are plenty of other valid reasons to chase the shiny ball to the next big idea, but keep in mind that if you move on frequently and find that you're feeling a little disappointed in yourself for not finishing enough projects, then a solution might be to consider two things:

1. Whether you're hovering within your creative essence, and

2. Who you are creating for.

This might help you pinpoint why you aren't completing projects.

Ultimately, whether to follow the shiny ball or not is completely your call. There are so many ways the shiny ball can help you or be a nuisance. If you need to develop your skills, find your style, or charge your energy, following the shiny ball can be an amazing tool for developing or helping your creative expression. Just do what feels best in a given moment, and try to enjoy it.

6

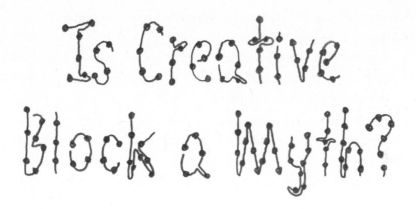

Is Creative Block a Myth?

Sometimes,
        there's just nothing.

There's almost no question
you've found yourself in this
conundrum: it's time to work.
all your creative tools are at
hand, you're free of
distractions...

        ...and the ideas just
                won't
                come.

There are times when I find myself staring at a blank page, a canvas, a screen—whatever is in front of me—and I hear the proverbial crickets. No ideas, nothing. In an effort to spark some energy, maybe I get up and turn on some music to pump myself up, or I'll browse online for something to inspire me. And still. Nothing.

At this point I reorganize my work space or go on a walk to look at the beauty in the world—this always leads somewhere, doesn't it? But still *nothing . . . nothing.*

NOTHING!

Despite all the years I've spent exploring the idea of creativity and developing art for a living, I have suffered from creative block on a handful of occasions. I've even enjoyed the sheer deer-in-the-headlights pleasure of trying to come up with a brilliant idea on the spot with dozens of people's eyes on me, when I've been totally frozen, unable to locate a singular thought in my brain (except a private, resounding scream: *COME ON, PHIL, THEY'RE ALL EXPECTING YOU TO COME UP WITH THE COOLEST IDEA IN THE UNIVERSE BECAUSE YOU'RE THE EXPERT ON CREATIVITY!*). Is that creative block? In the moment, it sure feels like it.

When people ask me whether creative block is really a thing, my answer may be a little unexpected. "I hope it's real!" I tell them. Sometimes it's the only explanation. I know a lot of people who come up with idea after idea and never seem to get stuck, but that's just not the case for most of us. How do you deal with it when it happens to you? The better question is actually: *How can you generate more ideas?*

I've learned that trying to understand why I'm experiencing creative block in any given moment can be frustrating, because the answer is different every time and across different circumstances. A few years ago, I set out to find a formula to discover what factors are needed for our creative output to flow. Rather than looking for things that block creativity, it made sense that if I could pinpoint every factor that's required to have creative output, I'd have a fighting chance at finding the antidote.

I made lists. I read tons of books and articles. I talked with friends, colleagues, clients, teachers from my past. Then I took everything I learned and distilled it into the simplest understanding possible to describe what's needed for consistent creative product:

$$\text{Skills + Ideas + Motivation = Output}$$

This encompasses both the quality of your art and the quantity you produce. Creative block shows up in any time, place, or circumstance, but I've discovered that any time it does, it's because at least one of these three elements is lacking.

You may have a *great idea* and be *super motivated* to make your project a reality—but then you realize you don't have the *technical skills* to bring it to life.

$$\boxed{\text{Skills + Ideas + Motivation = Output}}$$

Or you may have the *technical skills* to execute a project and be *motivated* to do it—but you can't come up with the *right idea* to work on.

$$\boxed{\text{skills} + \text{I}\cancel{\text{deas}} + \text{Motivation} = \cancel{\text{Output}}}$$

Most of us have experienced one of these circumstances—but the most common reason for creative block is as old as time itself: a *lack of motivation.*

$$\boxed{\text{skills} + \text{Ideas} + \text{Moti}\cancel{\text{vation}} = \cancel{\text{Output}}}$$

Sometimes motivation can come easily. For example, when you have to meet a deadline, you may be more likely to systematize a routine so that you're consistently showing up to your project and feeling ready to work. But have you ever met someone who is extremely creative and talented, but they never seem to fulfill their potential? If you've ever wondered how this can be, the odds are they just don't have the motivation that's necessary to act on their talent and/or their desire to create.

There are always exceptions to the rule. However, for the most part, creative thinkers need real, life-affecting motivation in order to produce their great ideas. When nothing tangible is hinging on a project's success, generating the motivation to finish it can be the most difficult challenge of all. Even if you have the skills and the ability to come up with fantastic ideas, without something (or someone) pushing you, your ideas will likely stay on the drawing board.

Introducing the least sexy chart of all time! But it's a worthwhile illustration of how you need all three elements working in

Creative Output

Motivation

Skills

Inspiration

unison to have consistent creative output. Remember: they don't have to pull equal weight. They can vary in degrees of influence, depending on the project. So, the next time you are feeling stuck, consider whether one or more of these three factors is missing. Now your job is to pinpoint exactly which may be lacking. This is how you can jump-start that missing ingredient to get your creativity flowing again.

There are a few things you can do when you notice your creativity isn't firing quite right. Let's start with overcoming a lack of skills—because that's the easiest one to solve. If you're tackling a project but don't have the technical skills to make it a reality, then you may need to learn a new skill, switch methods of creation, or find a skilled partner to help make your dream a reality.

What about not having any good ideas? This is the curse of the creative person's journey, in part because there's just no universal answer to judging the quality of your own ideas. I hope this book is presenting you with a few hands-on steps you can take to shake your ideas loose. You can always ask your friends or take a poll among the people closest to you, but ultimately you are the only one who can decide if a particular idea is worth pursuing.

If you realize you already have the skills and plenty of great ideas but can't get motivated to do the work, that may tell you everything you need to know: now it's time to figure out what the heck would get you moving! If you know you've got a cool idea but you aren't acting on it, this may be a good time to reach out to your creative buddy. If you don't have that figure in place just yet, then voice your goal to someone who will agree to hold you accountable.

IT'S TIME TO FIGURE OUT WHAT THE HECK WOULD GET YOU MOVING!

We're the only ones responsible for making sure we step up and do what's necessary to reach our goals. Sometimes that means equipping ourselves with the right supporter. Hell— why not up the game and wager some cold hard cash that you'll actually do it? I don't necessarily condone gambling, but if you give your friend a check and tell them to mail it to one of the Kardashians if you don't follow through . . . then guess what? Now you have a reason to get serious.

PHIL IN THE CIRCLE   1038
65D CARSON LM 22
MINNEAPOLIS IL 55411
                              10/20/2020
                              _____
                                    Date
Pay to Kim Kardashian $ | 1,000 |
        One thousand of them   ____ Dollars

        if I don't do
Memo   a podcast   _____
206238499   6182456009   WHAAT

I've noticed that most people who identify as creative already have the skills to be creative, or they would have given up on their creativity a long time ago. I've also found that most creative thinkers are quite capable of coming up with new ideas, or they'd probably be doing something else. So, what's the common theme here? It all goes back to the formula: to create something, let alone something *great*, you have to be aware of what's missing. Then find a way to keep creating.

A colleague of mine has a unique answer to getting herself motivated. When she finds that she needs a boost to get started on something new, she bakes something, *anything*—whether it's a batch of muffins for the week made with oatmeal and raisins, or something way simpler, like brownies from a boxed mix. She explained that the motions of pouring, mixing, and cracking the eggs can get her inspiration flowing, as if she's some kind of creative wizard. I'm sure we all can agree that a box of Duncan Hines does not a magician make, but it's not unusual for us creatives to seek out the easy ways to ramp up our oomph before we get down to work.

When my well gets a little dry or when I'm not feeling incredibly interested in what I'm supposed to be working on, I take a super long walk. The only "must" is that it's got to stretch beyond two hours. For some reason around the ninety-minute mark, the walk becomes rather hypnotic, Zen, and almost like meditating. When I come out of it, I feel totally refreshed and ready to get back to it. (Or I take a good nap first, and then get back to it.)

I know that everyone wants to know the premixed formula for beating creative block. The truth is, there is no universal answer—but you will definitely need all three of these elements pulling their weight. If you find you're lacking in any one of these, dig deep inside and find a solution that works for you, whatever it takes.

7

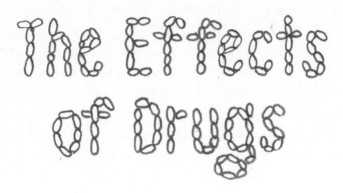

As I write this, I'm thinking about an old high school friend who had attention-deficit disorder. He was a little different because he would only take his medication when he needed to focus on studying for a big test. I remember thinking at the time: *Whoa. I wonder how much art I could get done if I could focus endlessly.* But instead I focused on taking every opportunity to work rather than trying to get it all done in one shot. I believe my work developed better this way, working bit by bit.

Creative types famously have a long and rough history with drugs and alcohol, from musicians like Kurt Cobain and Amy Winehouse to rebellious writers like Edgar Allan Poe, Philip K. Dick, and Hunter S. Thompson, but didn't they all die before their time? After hearing all the legendary stories about infamous creatives using drugs while making their art, it's easy to assume that drugs or alcohol will somehow help us on our creative journeys.

But is that really true, or do some artists just randomly stumble upon making sublime art while high AF, and then we all hail them as visionaries?

Can it be both?

One thing's for sure: our society views this differently now than it has in the past. Today, we see states legalizing weed, grandmas smoking blunts, researchers studying psychedelics, and the military experimenting with electric brain stimulation (while not a drug, it can have a similar effect). In addition, millions of otherwise drug-free people abuse prescription medications like Adderall to increase their productivity at work. With this national conversation going on, I wonder if drug use will eventually become widely accepted as part of the creative process. And if so, should it? Shouldn't we be looking for that spark elsewhere? Whenever I think of drugs and creativity, here is what I see from an outsider's perspective.

THE LEGENDARY UPSIDE OF CREATING ON DRUGS

Clearly, the biggest benefit of creating on drugs is that it changes an artist's state of mind. Drugs may cause a tightly wound (or super-self-critical) artist to ease up on their mental filtering of ideas. But there are many other means of easing up on ourselves. The first step is to simply give ourselves a break! Some artists claim to generate more ideas while they're on drugs. But I believe we can have the same effect if we intentionally write down all our ideas, however mundane or crazy, and work on developing them.

Some artists have also used drugs as a tool to increase their motivation to produce art. Some people find themselves manically creating on certain drugs like stimulants or hallucinogens. These are the drug-fueled creative sessions that legends are made of. Jack Kerouac wrote *On the Road* in three days while he was high on Benzedrine. David Bowie was so whacked out on cocaine for years, he had no memory of recording his hit record *Station to Station*. The list goes on. Some people may think that they can ape these moves, but the odds are pretty good that they will just think about all the great things they could be doing and then not do them . . .

THE SQUALID DOWNSIDE OF CREATING ON DRUGS

Of course, the biggest problem with taking drugs is they can royally screw up your life plan. Once some people sample the unusual feelings that drugs give them, they want more of that unusual feeling. This is when people find themselves beyond any useful effects of drugs and doing drugs becomes simply about doing drugs.

While drugs may inspire some new/creative ideas to pop into an artist's brain, with a little too much of the drug, an artist's entire workflow can fall apart. For starters, an artist's technical skills may begin to degrade, or drug use may sap their motivation, causing them to sit around and do nothing (instead of creating art, like they should). But the biggest problem is drugs can become an artist's crutch. I knew a painter in college who would get really high and paint until the sun came up. When I asked her about her process, she claimed she needed drugs to create. (I remember thinking, *I'm too poor for that!*)

In the end, our creativity is so delicate, it needs a perfect balance of motivation, skills, and ideas to sustain itself throughout our lives. If I had to choose between drugs or no drugs, I would definitely lean away and work on my skills. If you've dipped your toe into drugs and enjoy some of the positive effects, consider pulling back and see if you can replace what drugs give you by a more natural means. Work toward being more creative in your core and not looking toward something outside of yourself to get there.

Instead of saying "Yes, please!" to drugs, why not ask yourself, *How else can I achieve that feeling I'm looking for? Is there a non-chemical, non-addictive way I can convince my mental filter to let some of my wildest ideas through? Can I improve my motivation naturally?* Everyone is so different—find what works for your creativity. Speaking of, it's 6:00 a.m. Time for some coffee—the only drug I rely on to stimulate my productivity.

8

Success and failure are the same thing

Years ago, one of my art series was considered a big ugly fail-ure—by me. I created a series of fifteen works that went absolutely nowhere, which kind of messed with my head. I had assumed that those days were behind me—the times when every time a project flopped, I fell into a well of despair. But not so much.

When the series finished, I took a deep breath and tried to walk away . . . but as much as I attempted to shake it off, the feeling of failure lingered. Then, a few years later, I'd just been hired for a big commission project. I asked the client how they found me, and they mentioned that they'd loved one of my creations that they'd found online: one from this failed series that had haunted me for years!

That's when I made a game-changing discovery about my career: that old art series wasn't an ugly failure. It had a beautiful silver lining. Even though I didn't know it, it had helped me land a great client I never would have gotten without that series in my fail pile. Now, years later, as I've racked up plenty more "successes" and more "failures," I've often wondered: are success and failure just stories that we tell ourselves? After ruminating on this, I've decided they're just social constructs—products of our sensitive egos—that don't mean anything unless we give them meaning.

Looking back at my career, what I find interesting is that projects can evolve into just the opposite of what they were intended to be. Over time, sometimes a success will be considered a disaster for whatever reason, or a failed project (like my art series) will be considered a success. It's all so fickle—how can we know for cer-

They celebrate you one second and disdain you the next and so I never took any of the celebration very seriously – I want my obituary to be mine, not yours.

- Ethan Hawke

tain what "success" really means if it can be temporary? Remember the early piece I told you about in which I karate chopped paint onto a canvas to make a painting of Bruce Lee? It was a hit when I created it, and I felt that made it successful—but

ARE SUCCESS AND FAILURE JUST STORIES THAT WE TELL OURSELVES?

these days, some folks could consider it to be an example of cultural appropriation. Now that I have that awareness, I suppose I could view it either way . . . but if I showed audiences a new method or appreciation for understanding art, I guess I'd still consider it a success.

If you share an art project online and it bombs, it can feel pretty crummy. The good news is that news cycles have a short memory! Give it time. Maybe that same project will get shared on social media in a few months and become a surprising viral hit. There are a million ways your art can find a second life, which should give every artist hope. There is no such thing as failure, since after every hit and miss, you have to move on and create more work anyway.

Nothing can stay up or down forever. We are all human. We artists all have to find a way to get through the highs and lows of the art life. I've found most professional artists put a ton of pressure on themselves to produce a kick-ass project every time—but your creation doesn't care what it's called by the outside world. Not every work has to be considered a zinger, a ringer, or a winner. It just exists as art. That's it.

The way that I've learned to keep my eye on the big picture is to set up my next project while working on my current one. That way, I'm always excited about what's coming next. It helps keep my creative drive engaged with new projects, instead of hinging my emotions on the success of my last project.

However you choose to deal with the mutable concepts of success and failure, you can't allow your creativity to get tied up with how any one project lands with the public. If, in time, you discover that one of your projects somehow jumps from your failure pile to your success pile . . . simply remember that feeling. Use it as inspiration. And never forget that the one thing this project has in common with every other project you've done is—*it always leads to the next project*. Trust your process and just keep on creating. Win or lose, dammit, you're still making art and loving it. (Mostly.) No matter what anyone thinks—especially you—that's the real win.

Part 3
Keep On
Keeping On

1

Expert Block

In life, and certainly by the time we've become established as artists, we like to think we know what we're talking about. We want to sound smart at parties. We think we're well informed and believe that we have an intelligent understanding of how things work in the world because (hello) having knowledge is beneficial as you walk the planet . . . and having it tends to give you credibility. Being an expert on a specific topic can be great for creativity because it may give you a deeper understanding of how life and art can work. But sometimes, we can learn so much about a subject that we can become a little *too sure* of our own supreme intelligence and we begin to suffer from what I call "expert block."

Simply put, expert block is a notion that holds that the more we learn, the less open we are to new ideas. (Others might call this being a purist or an unintentional know-it-all.) If you aren't sure if you are afflicted by expert block, consider these symptoms:

» You suspect you sound like a know-it-all when talking about a particular subject.

» Your response to other people's creative ideas is an immediate "That will never work!"

» Your creative work has slowed down because you think, *What's the point? There's nothing left to do. I've done it all.*

» You've quietly said to yourself, "How do young people keep doing it?"

» You're surprised when someone else comes up with an idea you haven't thought of before.

If you can see yourself in any of the above symptoms, you may have expert block. I realize that being creatively blocked because you have "too much" knowledge sounds counterintuitive. You would think that if you knew a lot about a topic you would be great at solving problems and having insights around that topic. And sometimes, that's true—but on the flip side, sometimes all that knowledge can get in the way of growth and improvement. Being an expert often means you stop asking as many questions and stop seeking new solutions to problems, which can lead to a reduction in overall curiosity and exploration. So, Mister or Miss Expert over here ends up with fewer new life experiences, which is pretty terrible for a creative thinker. And if you ask me, becoming a card-carrying expert is the worst thing you can do for your

ALL THAT KNOWLEDGE CAN GET IN THE WAY OF GROWTH AND IMPROVEMENT.

creativity. Not to mention, most know-it-alls are often stuffy jerks. Have you noticed? Usually everyone around them has.

Last year, I was completely consumed by shiny ball syndrome and got taken up with etching, so I decided to try it out. I went into an art store to buy supplies but wasn't sure what I needed. I asked the guy behind the counter and was taken aback when he sarcastically replied, "Oh, so you're going to teach yourself how to etch and be the next Rembrandt?"

I laughed, because it was the only reply I could think of. As I asked him my questions, I learned that he had a degree

NO MATTER HOW GOOD YOU GET AT YOUR WORK, AVOID LETTING ALL THAT KNOWLEDGE GO TO YOUR HEAD.

in printmaking and thought it was cute when people tried to teach themselves. Patronizing much? Imagine a salesperson judging your curiosity to the point you feel a tiny bit stupid. I figured maybe he was having a bad day and searched my way into the appropriate aisle, where I bought some supplies so I could give it a shot.

It might be tough, but no matter how good you get at your work, avoid letting all that knowledge go to your head. If you feel your creativity is calcifying because you're just too damn experienced, that could actually be a sign of boredom. There are a few methods you can use to jog yourself out of expert block.

The first trick is to hold on to your enthusiastic wonder about the world. *Never let that go.* It will help you stay connected with your novice mindset (which we never want to lose) and keep the natural curiosity inside of you stoked. Even when you're a legit expert, thinking like a novice allows you to break the rules that a less experienced artist didn't even know existed, so you're increasing the chance of solving problems creatively.

Developing a novice mindset is all about tapping into your

own curiosity. It keeps you questioning, exploring, and looking at things in a new light, even when you think you know a lot about a topic already. If you've lost touch with your curiosity, then try picking the brain of a curious rookie in your world. That'll help nudge you out of your normal thinking patterns.

And even if you have the smallest question about something, don't assume you alone can figure out the answer. Asking questions is a skill you have to practice early on and continue to practice throughout your career. If you know a curious person you admire, try to identify exactly how, why, and where they see things differently. Then explore those avenues for yourself.

Finally, if there are rules related to your area of expertise, try to understand why they exist. Ask yourself: *What would happen if those rules were broken or changed?* Some rules are impossible to break, but if you explore the possibility of breaking them, it might reveal something to you . . . and at the very least, it could be a lot of fun! Having a novice mindset really can have a transformational effect on your creative projects. Never stop finding new approaches to old problems, even when it feels a little crazy or overwhelming to go back to the drawing board. And remember that growth doesn't have to happen in a straight line.

Becoming a novice again may sound easy, but it's actually not. It takes discipline, and you have to constantly remind yourself that you can always learn something new. Always try to look at things from a different vantage point. You never know what exciting places those fresh perspectives will take you. When you can see the world through a newbie's eyes, it can lead to a lot of explorative adventures, new insights, and a lot of fun. If you're a sourpuss who's got it all figured out . . . where's the fun in that?

2

Luck, or the great events that seem to happen to us only by chance, is usually associated with things like trips to Vegas or playing the lottery—not making music, drawing, or writing novels. Luck isn't something that generally comes to mind when we're talking about creativity—though for all we talk about elbow grease, work ethic, and productivity, I do believe in career luck. This can play a huge role in career-defining moments like being discovered by someone famous or finally getting your big break after you've toiled for years in anonymity.

I've often thought I was "crazy lucky" to have had one of my early art videos featured on the front page of YouTube back when the entire world saw the same landing page. Back then, over sixty thousand videos were uploaded per day. Somehow, mine was the one chosen. Well, sort of somehow. Like everyone else in the world at that time, I wanted my videos to be featured on YouTube's home page. One morning, I'd posted a video of a work that I'd produced that took a ton of effort and time . . . and it only got fifty views. I was wondering how YouTube chose which videos they featured, so I started hunting around for some info. Eventually, I found the YouTube blog where they had a post about how to get featured on their landing page. It was all about their principles of making a good video and the importance of not uploading copyrighted content. Not quite what I was looking for.

With a little browsing, I found a post that said YouTube was going to use guest curators to choose the videos that would be featured on the site. I started researching each of those curators until

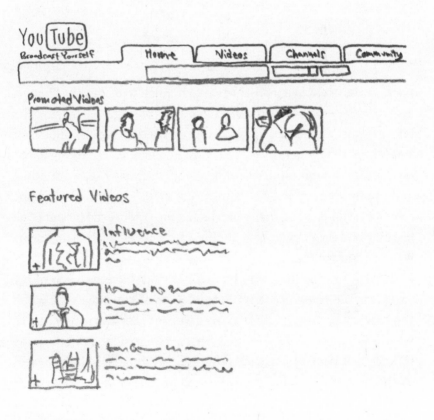

I found that one of them mentioned on their personal website that they were picking videos that same week.

So, I crafted an innocent introductory email and sent it to the curator. I also reached out to a random dude who had commented on the video that I wanted more viewers to see. Since he seemed interested in my work, I asked him to message the curator as well. He indulged me. That must have been enough, because the curator watched my video and shot me an email to notify me that she was going to feature it.

I still feel like it took some crazy luck, plus some notable marketing legwork, to make happen—but this is how active you have to be in making your luck build. In the end, it can play a powerful role in your life.

There are thousands of nuanced ways luck can influence our careers, but most of them fall into two broad categories: setting the stage and the stage (of life).

SETTING THE STAGE

The first type of luck is embedded in our upbringing. Before we venture out into the world, we tend to be affected by early influences like parents, teachers, and friends. When we grow up surrounded by a group of people who support our creative endeavors, we are experiencing the "luck of an emotionally supportive base," probably without even realizing it. A supportive base can provide us with the confidence to keep pursuing our creativity into our adult lives, which to many people could be considered a lucky break.

You may also experience something called the "luck of geography" without realizing it. Growing up in a big city that exposes you to all kinds of great art at museums and theaters, creative people, and different cultures can positively influence your creative expression in so many ways. Compare that to growing up in a rural logging community, where there are far fewer displays of creativity (and creative outlets) and you can see how being raised in a large city could be considered lucky.

Looking back on my childhood, my greatest stroke of luck was that I had emotionally supportive parents who encouraged my art projects. Lucky, right? But there are also times when I find myself pausing before I pursue certain controversial art projects, simply because I think my parents might find them offensive. A mindset like that is not good for one's creativity. I still think of my parents as providing a strong base for my creative expression—but if I shift my perspective just a degree or two, I could also say their unwavering support has hindered my ability to push the boundaries of my art.

Conversely, I have a friend who had unsupportive parents. They told her that pursuing an art career was a waste of time. Was this bad luck for her? It could easily be interpreted that way. But for my friend, this wasn't bad luck at all! Her parents hating on her artistic dreams actually helped liberate her creatively. Seeing she had no support at home, it motivated her to follow her own path. I think her luck came in the form of having a personality that doesn't give a damn what other people think.

THE STAGE (OF LIFE)

As adults, when something "lucky" happens to us, we tend to be aware of what actually took place for that fortuitous moment to occur, mainly because a lucky break means you're usually getting some kind of tangible reward. Say you're a designer, and one of your Instagram followers happens to work for a company that you'd love to collaborate with. You connect with your follower, they're thrilled to hear from you, they get what you're trying to do, and they help you land that job. Was that luck or networking?

Let's say you're in a punk band in college, and your dad mentions that one of his clients at the corporation where he works is looking to hire a band to record some original background music with a punk rock flair for a commercial. You may prefer to stay punk rock forever and not "sell out" to the man . . . but you also need the money to fix your tour van. So, you record a track that gets you some cash to get back on the road and perform for your fans.

When it comes to interpreting luck in our lives, most people tend to lean in one of two ways. Either a person will totally ignore the role good fortune plays and lay claim to all the big things that happened to them, or they'll acknowledge that they sometimes get lucky and will look to conjure more luck in their lives. Personally? I'm in the latter group. It helps my creativity if I think of luck as some force out there that's just waiting to sit on my shoulder. This view reduces some of the pressure I put on my own creativity. If I felt I was in total charge of my fate, I might see success and failure in a much more personal way.

If you feel you've been living under an upside-down horseshoe lately, I have only one recommendation: *keep your horizons wide open.* When you keep your world open to new opportunities, whatever shape they may take, you're likely to encounter more lucky breaks. The wider the lens, the more opportunities you'll have to spot those moments—even if they're far off in the distance and don't look like you thought they would. When you want to grow your career, don't consider yourself too cool for anything. Some of the opportunities that seemed lowest profile actually led to some of my biggest chances.

There were also events in my journey that appeared lucky, but behind the scenes they were actually a solid mixture of luck and working my butt off. A prime example was in 2012, when I was part of a worldwide talent search that TED ran. They opened up the possibility for anyone in the world to apply to speak at TED. As I recall, they wanted to find twelve people who had never spoken before to give a talk, and I think they asked TED employees to message people they knew who might have a story to share.

I had no idea what was coming when a guy who worked in the engineering department at TED in the UK emailed me. He said he was a fan of my work and wondered if I had a story to share. I thought about it for a bit. To be honest, this wasn't the kind of thing I was looking for. I was an artist and had never been on-stage. But in keeping my horizons wide open, I thought I should look into it—especially when I considered the limitations I had been exploring.

I wondered if maybe I could bring that into a narrative. I began to work at it, putting together a one-minute video application. With that, I was accepted. Then I was selected to go to New York and give a four-minute talk. At this point, I had never spoken on a stage in my life. The odds of being chosen were quite low. There were over three hundred people worldwide chosen to give four-minute talks.

A couple of months later, TED posted all those four-minute talks online. Each speaker was the only person who received the link, and my task was to get as many views as possible. Again, I worked my butt off and shared the link with about twelve thousand people. I also asked them to share it with friends. Well, people shared and I got super lucky and the talk went viral.

It's one instance of how luck played out in my career—a lot of stars had to line up just right. And by the way, this opportunity still wasn't a shoo-in for me. Since the TED organizers were only planning on inviting twelve speakers from around the world, I knew I still had a slim chance at making the cut, but I believed I was in the mix.

I sat and I waited. The date of notification came and went, and I accepted that I probably hadn't been chosen. Then the organizers reached out to say they were delayed in making their decision . . . then a few days later, I got the invite. At the time I couldn't even fully understand how big of a deal this was for my life.

Considering all the work that went into making the TED stage, why should we talk about luck at all? If you can view your life through a broad lens and start each day with a wide-open view for how your creative dreams could possibly manifest and then consistently put yourself to the task and work hard at it, luck can help guide you to a lot of unexpected opportunities. And call it what you like, but unexpected opportunities are always welcome, for any career!

LUCK IS AS MUCH ABOUT PASSION AND COURAGE AS IT IS ABOUT THE STARS ALIGNING FOR YOU.

In the end, luck is as much about passion and courage as it is about the stars aligning for you. The ability to stay devoted to your art, along with your willingness to take risks for your work (and in your work), are just as great as any good fortune.

3

Just a Little Bit Insane

One thing I've found that a lot of professional creatives mutter to themselves is, "I had to be crazy to think I could make a living doing this!" When we reflect on our early days, many artists will think we must have been delusional to keep trying to "make it."

I've found that early on in your creative endeavors, having a little irrational confidence in your art can actually help you get through the growing pains of being an artist (or at any point in your art career, really). If you logically look at the prospects of making a living in the arts, it's kind of an insane decision to even attempt. That's why I think a little bit of craziness can actually *help* an art career.

The most common crazy thing we do is sacrifice all of life's modern luxuries just to succeed in the arts. The term "starving artist" had to come from somewhere, right? It's because many of us are willing to give up certain basics so we can spend that money buying supplies for things we want to create. (Sanity be damned!) We often refer to this as "following our dreams" or being "passionate," but I think of it as a beautiful delusion.

The crazy can play out in so many ways. I've seen comedians play to a silent room and exit stage left bragging that they killed it when most of the laughs they got were due to being laughed *at*. I've seen artists show their work at fairs every month, just hoping

A LITTLE BIT OF CRAZINESS CAN ACTUALLY HELP AN ART CAREER.

more buyers will approach, while they're essentially losing money. And I've seen musicians play the same coffee shop for a decade. Please remember, I do not criticize. After all, these reflections come from the guy who for years relied on frozen burritos for sustenance.

Looking back, I've been delusional, pragmatic, and lucky to make a career out of my creativity. But my blissful insanity has been replaced by flashes of anxiety. Sometimes I wake up in the middle of the night and wonder, *How the hell am I going to keep this up my entire life? This week, my life seems on track . . . but a year from now? Five years from now?*

The truth is, almost every human being on the planet—even those with *the most* secure jobs—could face this same reality. Others like me have proven to themselves that they can get the work. The greater skill is putting enough trust in the universe that those future projects will come. Is this potentially a little crazy self-talk? Okay, yes. And a little of that can be a good thing.

If your loved ones express concern about your work because they're afraid for your well-being, try not to let that hurt your feelings—and try not to hurt theirs. However, don't give up on your dreams. Instead, try to understand where they're coming from. They're looking out for you. There was that recent frozen burrito recall, and they feel maybe you've just taken this whole maker-for-life thing a little too far. Not only is it important to see your life choices from other perspectives, but it can actually serve your art well. The ability to flip between logic and slightly delusional thinking will be good for your art, and maybe even help you discover the hard-to-see next steps that can help you achieve your creative goals.

Even if you're not laughing all the way to the bank 100 percent of the time, make sure you're laughing as you walk away from the bank 100 percent of the time. Gotta keep the crazy alive.

4

Commercial Success Kills Creativity

We all have our favorite bands. When one of mine drops something new, I can't help getting excited. This happened recently when the singer of a metal band I love released some new tracks. But as I downloaded and listened, I went from excited to . . . bewildered . . . because I found myself suddenly listening to dance music. What happened to the metal? The new songs weren't bad, but I had to fight back disappointment and remind myself: "She's an artist! She explores!" I had flubbed by expecting an artist's current work based on their past. I should've known better than to believe that every commercially established artist should explore the one idea that made them famous, ad infinitum. The reality is that's just not how most artists think.

Most creative people prefer to explore their art to its limits. They may try all kinds of styles, ideas, and methods of expression in their careers. But after experiencing some commercial success, many people feel pressure to continue making more of that "successful" material. Our culture's obsession with commodifying art often persuades popular artists away from exploring their pure artistic vision. That's because over time, as we continue to repeat themes and ideas, our work grows less creative or original because creativity and success are often two totally different pursuits. It's still art, but it's less creative. Controversial opinion? Maybe. But when I make art with a repeated theme and material, it's inherently less creative than the first time I did it. But this doesn't change its definition as art.

WHAT? you might think. *How can commercial success hurt my creativity?* I like to describe how it feels to sell your first work of art. When you make something for the first time, it's full of your pure creative energy because it's the first of its kind. But when you're asked over and over to make something similar to your past hits because people can't get enough of it, your creativity naturally declines because there are fewer new elements to explore. When you create a similar work for the fifth or five hundredth time, you may still enjoy doing it (probably because art is your passion), but the process will be less creative than the first time you did it. It's that simple. These replicated works are still meaningful, marketable, and desirable to many people, but the artist will often feel that something is lacking—*because something is.* This isn't a huge deal for every creative (hey, commerce exists), but for artists who want to keep their creativity sharp, it can be a real problem.

CREATIVITY AND SUCCESS ARE OFTEN TWO TOTALLY DIFFERENT PURSUITS.

To counteract this, I suggest commercially successful artists consider going the "one for them, one for me" route. While you're making more work that's just like your old hits, experiment with

Over the years I have watched so many other people murder their creativity by demanding that their art pay the bills.

- Elizabeth Gilbert

new things, too. The beauty of this approach is that you can sell those familiar works while constantly exploring new avenues, which could lead you to new hits. You might decide to totally re-invent your art every few years. Just know that whenever you make a major shift in your aesthetics, it may be harder to sell your work than before because you'll probably have to find new fans for each of your distinct styles. But who cares solely about commerce? No matter how many units you sell, you can't ignore your creativity and just keep knocking out rehashes of old pieces to make your mainstream fans happy. If you do have to pay the bills with your art, then well done for having reached the point where your creativity contributes to at least a portion of your income. Just make sure your art is always yours.

Success is a coup for any artist. I desire it. You probably do, too. But if we want to stay creative for a lifetime, it's worth paying attention to how much we shape-shift our creative ideas just to gain commercial success. I'm guilty of having typecast myself in some ways, just to have an art career. But guess what my goal for the next five years is?

I want to fail more.

Risking failure helps keep your creativity from stagnating, so you're not falling into the success loop and "selling out" your creativity for the almighty dollar. Because here's the least shocking news you'll read all day: piles of money never make an unfulfilled artist happy. Only piles of surplus creativity will. Your mind is your greatest commodity. Keep investing there.

5

Give an Artist a Break, and While You're at It, Give Yourself a Break

"Imagine a world . . ."

Are you getting my film trailer voice-over vibe? But really: think how lovely it would be if we lived in a world where an individual who couldn't find something nice to say would say nothing at all.

I know I'm probably dreaming of some civilization that never existed. But these days, I think many of us would agree that it often seems like the least-informed people are the ones who shout the loudest. Why do some people feel entitled to oink their opinions at others every chance they get? This irresistible desire to critique another person's life, appearance, talent, or work fascinates, befuddles, and often discourages me—not only because I'm an artist, but because I care about other humans.

This unconstructive criticism trend, a.k.a. trolling, has become a pastime that allows each of us to witness a lot of the criticism that used to happen exclusively in the privacy of an individual's mind. It's no wonder so many young people live with anxiety. The second you share yourself with the world, you've also put yourself out there like a volunteer inside a dunking booth. There's no thought or feeling that's sacred enough to make others think twice before taking aim at us.

And when you're an artist, enduring this isn't so much an elective choice as a way of life. Maybe we should be used to being critiqued, but put simply, the meanness we encounter just hurts. Our drawing skills are judged by our peers as early as kindergarten, far before we've even gained all our motor skills, which can be so terrifying it causes some kids to start stress-eating crayons (just kidding). The same thing happens in middle school and then high school—why do you think we artists clutch our sketchbooks so close to our chests? Those books are full of our most personal thoughts and feelings. Heck, they are really parts of our souls.

Sharing art with someone else is an inherently vulnerable experience. Particularly for those of us who are shy, it takes a ton of guts to put our work out there. When our work gets trashed, it stings, often way more than most people know. Good or bad, genius or hot garbage, every piece we make is an extension of who we are. So, why are people so tough on artists?

You never know whose hopes and dreams you're casually torpedoing the next time you @ someone with some poison-penned hot take. Growing up, I was fortunate to have parents who never uttered a negative word about my art, even though I could tell they didn't always get it. They recognized my work as my way of expressing who I was, which helped give me the confidence I needed not only to pursue an art career, but just to walk peacefully in the world. Sadly, many creatives never get this kind of support. Some will totally stop creating because of a rough critique or the cumulative effect of a bunch of bad reviews. Whenever I see this happen to another artist, it literally hurts me. "Don't listen to those people," I want to tell them. "Everyone hates something."

Some haters will disagree (because that's what they do), but I didn't write this chapter to complain on behalf of all artists. Boohoo, someone didn't like your work, ban all art criticism. No way. Criticism has tons of value, so it's necessary and can be useful for any artist. But we should encourage the world to try to think about what a particular artist was "going for" before trolling on, uninformed. Before we crap mightily all over any given artist's work, can we rephrase the criticism to focus on that particular piece without devaluing another human being? That's the difference, and it's not just in art. In everything we say to or about each other, don't hate on someone. We never know how much of an impact a comment can have on even the strongest individual. (And virtually every artist is a more sensitive type—you feel me?)

Instead of throwing hate grenades, try to help the artist improve by finding some element that you like about their piece. Ask them a question about it. And if you do truly hate some piece of art, you can always just allow the artist's own flagging self-esteem, confidence, and inner demons do the work for you! (That was a joke. *But it's kinda true.*)

For people who feel inclined to question or bash someone else's work, remember that silence is sometimes the most powerful feedback. Give an artist a break today. Hold off on that comment. Maybe not critiquing someone will brighten your day a smidge, too.

I'll openly admit that, honestly, I'm delicate. I shut down at criticism. If someone in my life criticizes me in a way that feels unreasonable, I get pretty hurt. I've learned that my best response is to just get to work on whatever is next. Little by little, this helps put it out of my mind. People say things. Most often they don't even remember. And if they don't remember, then in theory, maybe you and I should try to just let it slide as well. It's not easy, though. Our hearts are in our art.

After getting advice from several career artists I respect, I've also learned how to toughen up. These days I respond (and really believe): "Say whatever you want, trolls. I'll push through this and come out the other side with more durable skin and a defiant heart. Dammit." It's a healthy battle cry to get you pumped up to fight trolls.

On the flip side, see if you can recall the most hateful thing someone has ever said to you. It stings, doesn't it? Now think: *Have I ever spoken to myself in a way that's harsh, critical, shaming, or awful?* Of course you have. If you have a self-loathing bone in your body (and what creative person doesn't?), there is a good chance you've said far worse about yourself than anyone else ever could. When we enter a creative field, we find we're inherently surrounded by people to compare ourselves to. *Their studio is bigger than mine. They're better at painting. How did they come up with that?!* If you've ever heard the saying "Compare and despair," there's a lot of that going on for our type. As if our work isn't tough enough.

There have been many times when I've thought so little of myself, or my work, that I realized I was beating myself up. But does self-abuse ever jar loose any good ideas or help our confidence? Not at all. Ever. Take my word for it. It's the least productive thing.

When we tell ourselves that we suck, it lowers inspiration dramatically. That's why, as much as artists love to torture ourselves, I think we owe it to our art to *give ourselves a break*. If you're working on a challenging project and not seeing results, just relax, breathe, and step away from the action for a while. Remember: *how you feel is still just one person's opinion*. Even if it's yours. If you find you're taking your work too seriously, you're not allowing much of the good stuff to flow.

I know that just a few pages ago I encouraged you to let go of rules when it comes to your art, but here's one that we all need to hang on to: if you've beaten yourself so far down that a break won't cut it, try giving your creativity a *second chance*. Because as cut-throat as the arts can be at times, creating art is never a single-elimination Hunger Games tournament where the second-place prize is death. *Your art is allowed as many second chances as you will give it*. So, if you love creating, why not give yourself a second, third, or even a thirty-eighth chance to get that creative idea where you want it to go? Don't hesitate to ask someone about that hot new technology that you've been thinking is beyond your ability to use in your art. Don't believe that you'll never be smart enough to learn some complex skill. Try it. Most ideas are shit, remember? If a project doesn't work out the first time, hey, it happens. You got this.

Whether it is you getting yourself down or someone else trying to knock you down, get off your own back or get someone else off your back. Then get back to work.

6

Break It Down to Build It Up

Back in high school, a regional newspaper started publishing my cartoons on a weekly basis. It was the most amazing thing ever to happen at that point in my young career: all I did was walk into the paper's office and ask to speak with the person who was in charge of the comics page. The editor looked up from her desk, rather surprised to lay eyes on a high school kid with a binder full of cartoons under his arm.

She explained that she didn't have room on the comics page for my work, but she did have room on the teen page that was published once a week in the Lifestyle section of the paper. Needless to say, I was thrilled. I was being paid $25 a cartoon and had real dreams of being a professional cartoonist.

After a few months, my editor came to me. She and her colleagues felt I'd exceeded their initial expectations, and they were offering me a permanent spot on their comics page, producing a new cartoon every day. I'd proven myself on the teen page, she said. Now there was just one condition: "Can you really do it?" she said. "This isn't a job you can half-ass." I had a week to give her my answer, but I already knew. My dream was about to come true.

Until that moment, my method for coming up with cartoon ideas had always been pretty simple: I'd sit and wait for an idea to pop in my head. I never had an avalanche of great ideas in one day, but I felt confident that coming up with new ones wouldn't be a problem. I sat down and put on paper as many fun new concepts as I could.

At first, the task was easy . . . but after a couple days, I started to freak out. I wasn't coming up with many good ones. As the week wore on, I realized I wasn't going to be able to pull it off. I went in to see the editor and turned down the job. It was a complete bummer, and I got a little depressed about it.

Even to this day, it's one of the biggest letdowns I've experienced. In the years since, I've worked on creating methods to come up with fresh ideas when things aren't going quite my way. When analyzing the idea generation process, I've found that ideas seem to come to us in three distinct ways: spontaneous creativity, contemplative creativity, and systematic creativity.

There's some overlap between these three methods (because creativity can be murky like that). Let's put all three under the microscope so we know how to use them when our creative wellspring is spitting sand.

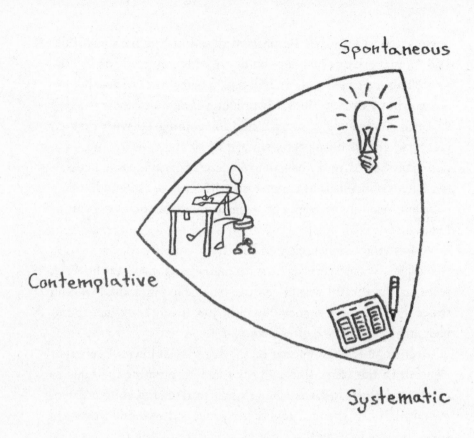

Spontaneous

Contemplative

Systematic

SPONTANEOUS CREATIVITY

This flashy form of idea generation is what gets all the attention. You're going about your day when, in a flash, a brilliant idea strikes. It's the classic light bulb over your head, the aha moment, the spark of insight. In America, we romanticize the hell out of the lone genius who comes up with brilliant ideas out of thin air. You see it all the time on the screen and on the page. Think back to *Mad Men*'s Don Draper coming up with the famous Coke commercial while meditating, and you'll understand how we lionize this form of idea generation in our culture.

What those stories don't tell you is that great ideas rarely come out of thin air. Spontaneous ideas are usually very well vetted! They're often connected to something you're currently working on or have previously worked on, or they are related to a subject you are already quite familiar with. For example, a professor of space  plasma physics probably won't come up with a new break-dance move, and a break-dancer probably won't come up with a new theory on earth's radiation belts.

I've found amazing spontaneous ideas can happen as often as a few times a day to as little as once every few months—so don't count on making a creative living by working off nothing but spontaneous ideas. Remember: no one has ever successfully bludgeoned themselves into coming up with a great idea. I tried with my cartooning, but see how it didn't work? You just can't force it. The truth is, you kind of have to mull it. Most ideas come as a direct result of *working* at it.

CONTEMPLATIVE CREATIVITY

This method of idea generation happens when you spend a lot of time seriously thinking about a creative solution or idea. Think of the artist's sketchbook that's full of drawings that explore a certain subject. Or the hours spent with a guitar discovering a new arrangement. It's the brainstorming meetings at work or the afternoons with a friend discussing a project in detail. When you explore an idea in a deliberate way, be sure to explore openly, without the pressure of arriving at an immediate answer. Sometimes "living in the question" for a while is a great method to allow the best ideas to bubble up.

After you contemplate like Rodin's *The Thinker*, know that a fully baked idea may come to you hours later like a thunderbolt of genius, because these methods love to overlap and play off each other. The reason why an amazing idea may spontaneously occur to you (hours or even days after a contemplative session) is because you've presented your brain with a problem to solve—so your unconscious mind continues trying to solve it, even when your conscious mind has moved on to other things.

SYSTEMATIC CREATIVITY

 If you want to push contemplative creativity to the max, this is where you end up: it's a process called systematic creativity. This method takes advantage of both spontaneous and contemplative creativity, and the results are often a wild cacophony of creative thoughts. It's often used when you are no longer simply thinking about an idea—you're actively analyzing a project you're working on like a mathematician, creating lists of all the possible permutations from each piece of the project, and then systematically combining elements together to see if anything interesting arises.

Systematic creativity looks different for each of us. It's the interior designer listing every variation of textures for all the elements in a room and mixing those possibilities up until something cool happens. It's the musician who wrote some great lyrics but is trying thirty different combinations of notes to see if something interesting happens when one combination is played as a process of nailing down the melody. Or it's the cartoonist looking at their old cartoons and making lists of what they see, and then combining those elements to see if a new idea strikes.

Systematic creativity takes a lot of time and always gives you plenty of garbage to sift through, but what's great about this process is it forces you to generate ideas, which is a huge step in the right direction. A systematic approach can be a fantastic tool for people in all kinds of environments. Many times, just the act of putting pen to paper or brush to canvas can be a sticking point for a lot of people—so being forced to write down your ideas, even if they suck or don't make sense, can be a good place to start. Systematic creativity is something I discovered (many years) after my cartoonist gig. I always thought of my cartooning stint as a minor failure, but looking back, it was simply a problem of not knowing how to generate ideas. You live, you learn, and you realize you've got more important things to dwell on than fearing you'll be a one-hit wonder. However you get there, just keep creating!

I Have an Idea

As I mentioned, I failed miserably at my teenage dream of becoming a professional cartoonist for the simple (and totally manageable!) problem of not being able to come up with enough ideas. Now I want to dig deeper into the idea of systematic creativity and make a little cartoon-generating exercise. Hopefully, what you'll get out of this is a couple of cartoons, a couple of laughs, and a process that may help you in the future with your own projects.

Let's start by analyzing some old cartoons I drew years ago. I'd like you to write down some of the things, places, and topics that are featured in the cartoons (and I'll do the same). Once we've created a list of topics, we'll look at the cartoons again and jot down smaller details that pertain to each topic. Lastly, we will mix and match some ideas from each list to see if it sparks anything new. If you get stuck, don't worry. I'll be here to walk you through the entire process.

Candle, wax museum

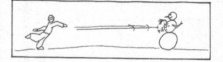

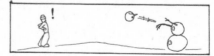

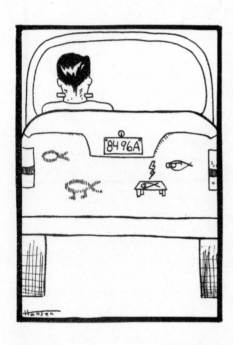

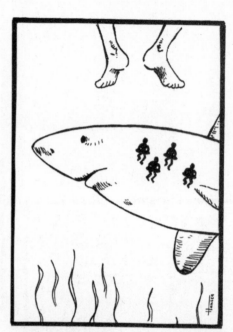

Step 1: Create Categories

I see all kinds of weird randomness here. I also see each cartoon has a subject, an action, and a possible location where the cartoon takes place. I can definitely spot some details that don't fit into a single category. Let's start with these categories: *subject, action, location,* and *bonus detail.*

Step 2: Fill in the Details

Now I'm going to fill each of my four main categories with specific details I see in the cartoons. I see some odd subjects—snowmen, candles, sharks, and cows. I also see actions like swimming, branding, and throwing. Some of the cartoons appear to take place at night or in winter. As for bonus details, I see a lot of random things like bumper stickers and reanimation. I went ahead and wrote down every detail I could find, and placed them in their appropriate category. Please do the same in the spots provided. Write down everything you see.

Subject	Action	Location	Bonus Detail
_____	_____	_____	_____
_____	_____	_____	_____
_____	_____		_____
_____	_____	_____	_____
_____	_____	_____	
_____	_____	_____	_____
_____	_____	_____	_____
_____	_____	_____	_____
_____	_____	_____	_____
_____	_____	_____	_____
_____	_____	_____	
_____	_____	_____	_____
_____	_____		

Step 3: Mix and Match

Now for the fun part—I want you to make a bunch of random connections between your categories. I'm going to work from left to right, selecting one word from each category, but do it however you want. There are no rules! You can combine multiple elements from the same category, or you can mix and match and put together any word combination you like. The only goal here is to create a bunch of random connections. Then we will use these connections to spark some ideas.

Subject	Action	Location	Bonus Detail
Snowman	Revenge	Car	Bumper sticker
Shark	Branding	Museum	Doggie Bag
Coroner	swimming	Winter	Headless
cow	throwing	Night	Driving
Frankenstein	Visit Museum	work	
Farmer	keeping score	Ocean	
Candle	Taking something home		

Step 4: What Ideas Did You Spark?

Based on my mixing and matching, you could use a bunch of these quirky connections to make a new cartoon. For instance, you could draw a cartoon of a shark putting bumper stickers in a museum. How about a cartoon of a cow and snowman swimming together? Maybe you imagine Frankenstein contemplating a higher power and remembering his late wife, "The Bride." Whatever you came up with, it doesn't have to make sense at first! As you think about them more, your brain will naturally filter things and hopefully you'll come up with a funny little cartoon idea. Go ahead and draw a few ideas here.

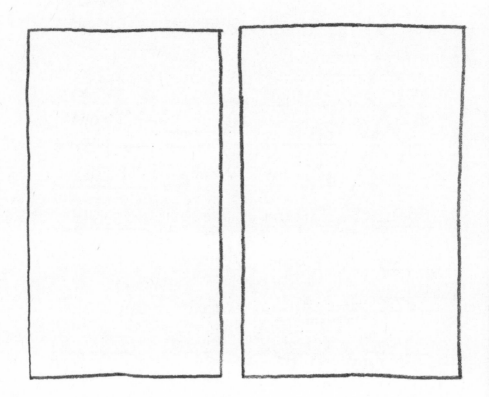

I spent a few minutes thinking about each of my combos, and this is what I came up with:

Cow Bumper Stickers

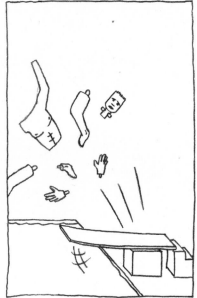

When Frankenstein hit the board at the Olympic Springboard finals, his dreams weren't the only thing to break apart.

It feels like a nice little collection to me—and I hope you can see how systematic creativity is an effective method for literally forcing the creativity out of you. Give it a shot the next time your idea generation isn't going according to plan. If you're a writer, take one element of your story and list ten other possible options, then see if any of them spark for you. If you're a painter and want a fun unexpected project, look at the last five pieces you created and see if you can combine or blend some of the elements in them (like we did here) and paint it. Try this even if it's not something you would normally do! Systematic creativity is a great way to look at idea generation from a totally different angle. It's also a fun way to create a weird Frankenstein project. Heck, you might discover something amazing along the way!

7

Ignoring the Data

Occasionally, some well-intentioned person will send me an article on how to be more creative. Thanks, I say—but does that mean it seems to them like my ideas are getting stale? At some point in an artist's career, it's likely that that's the case.

As a result, I've read hundreds of these articles looking for clues. What I discovered is that most of them *totally contradict each other.* One day I'll read something that claims: "New study shows people are more creative when they're not distracted—so clean your cluttered work space." Then I'll read one that says: "Study shows distractions keep minds active, so stock your work space with fun trinkets." What the heck?

This can get annoying if you take the insights seriously— because actually, *both claims are true.* The wild card in all this? It's you. Repeat after me: there is no magic bullet. Different stimuli work for different creative people. Something that ignites your

Become an Expert

DON'T LIMIT YOURSELF

be quiet

Put a plant in your workspace.

Use your opposite hand

Look

Try something NEW!

Take a nap

Reward your curiosity

Expect the unexpected

Be sarcastic

DARKEN YOUR WORK SPACE!

Find stimulation

Experience something aBsuRD

List problems Look

for

Make a collage

Don't multitask

Embrace a warm-up ritual

order

Sit in a coffee shop

Dance around the house

for opportunities to collaborate

walk the train

Rethink a label

Create a mind map

Take risks

in

Challenge YOURSELF

chaos

EXERCISE

KeepGapsBetween CreativeActionShort

Write ideas down

Work when you're tired

Have a deadline

Write songs to your pets

Create psychological distance
Let go of expectations
Be sarcastic
Work when you're tired
Daydream
Don't be afraid to make a msitake
MEDITATE
LIMIT YOURSELF
Break out of established patterns
Create a Treasure chest
Don't expect perfection
Take a
Be social
Listen to music
Spend time alone
GET Silly
Switch off your inner critic.
Visit a foreign country
Walk
Stop watching TV
Write by hand
Dim the lights
Don't have a deadline
Practice Practice Practice
Free-associate
DO WHAT YOU LOVE
Create an inspiration board
Get someone else's opinion
Gesture More
Free Write
Work from a different way
Laugh!
Drink
Play video games
Be anti-social
Do
Lie down

> An underrated thing that you can do that no one does anymore, just sit in a dark room. Give yourself like 20 minutes, don't meditate, actually think about things. I feel like if you have a bunch of problems in your life, it's amazing how 20 minutes alone in the middle of the day in a dark room can change everything.
>
> – Chuck Klosterman

creativity today may not be what gives you a spark tomorrow, and something that aids your career tomorrow may just be a stepping-stone for your much longer travails. Don't get too hung up on any of the "facts."

You will never need to read another "How to Be More Creative" article for the rest of your life, but you may find this next section handy. I've pored over countless articles and research papers on the subject, and boiled them down to my own list of "68 Tips to Boost Your Creativity." The next time you're in a creative rut, try a few and see which ones work for you. Before you begin, keep in mind you are not looking for a storm of brilliant ideas to rain down on you, but rather for your mind to simply feel reinvigorated and more responsive to new ideas.

In the coming months, as you try an idea here or there, take note and add the ones that worked to your bag of tricks. Many on this list are passive moves designed to change your environment, or minor adjustments you can make to your brain to be more receptive to new ideas. To make them easier to classify, I've created three broader categories that I feel many of these tips fall under. So, the next time you need to give your creativity a little shake, you will know which of these three situations you're currently experiencing, and you can try all the moves in that category.

Okay, here we go!

1. **Change It Up.** These techniques put you in a receptive mental state without a specific goal. It's best to practice them when you want to feel an overall boost in creativity but don't have a specific goal in mind. They aren't meant to solve a creative problem but rather to put you in a more creative mindset. Examples: take a nap, experience something absurd, eat mashed potatoes with your hands, laugh for five minutes, or quit watching Netflix.

2. **Tweak Your Process.** These techniques are good for making slight adjustments to a creative task that is already in progress. These tips include: create psychological distance from your project, create a false deadline, intentionally change the way you work, or brainstorm. They're excellent to use when you have a project that's going pretty well, but you want to alter your approach a little to see if your work can get even better.

3. **Get Analytical.** Like the second category, you can di-

rectly apply these moves to a project you are working on midstream. They include: analyze your assumptions, create a flowchart, outline new paths, and reimagine the problem. I realize getting super analytical on your creative challenges can seem counterintuitive, but these are great to use when you're waist-deep in a project and need all the good ideas you can get.

Your challenge now is to fill in these three boxes with specific techniques that work for you. Keep in mind, your custom approach must be uniquely yours or the tips will be useless when you need them most. A sculptor will probably not write down "use your hands" on any list, since that's an essential part of sculpting—right? But someone who spends all day on a computer might love it. A quiet librarian may get a phenomenal creative boost by laughing for five minutes straight—but a comedian who is constantly surrounded by laughter may not. See why customization is so important?

When you simply need a creative boost, refer to your personal list.

Change It Up

Tweak Your Process

Get Analytical

Idea # 69

Cut this page out and tape to something
soft like a pillow, balloon, or sweater.

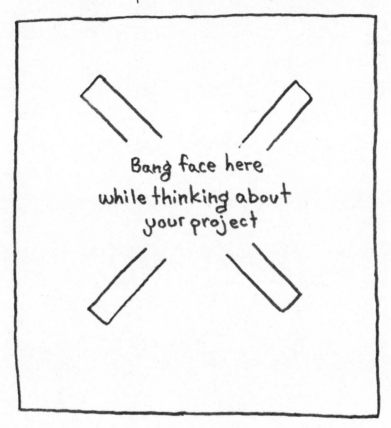

Bang face here
while thinking about
your project

Are you thinking differently yet?
If not, just know you look
hilarious doing it.

8

Every artist may not be a Rhodes Scholar, but most creative thinkers I know are hyper-curious information sponges who love to
learn new things. This often bleeds into our creative work. Think
of the garage band drummer with a green thumb who becomes so
fascinated with her garden that she makes videos where she turns
plants into percussive instruments. Or the young oil painter who
is introduced to screen printing and begins using it to make more
replicas of her work to sell to her fans. Anything you learn in life
has the potential to become creative material for you.

I know it can be tempting for students in a creative field to
graduate and just stop learning. School's out forever, so there's
nothing left to learn . . . right? Well, yes *and* no. Yes, creatives **can**
leave behind all those standardized tests that were clearly written
by noncreative muggles and skip all those classes that forced us to
learn things we'll never use. But no, we should never stop learning

if we want to produce great art. Constantly learning is essential for any person—but if you're an artist, I feel like you have an even greater obligation to continue your education. This is how you will begin to see the world in a more nuanced way, which will help you create more intelligent and nuanced art. But wait—*there's more.*

Learning more about the world helps to spark your curiosity, which leads to more creative ideas. I do this all the time. Every artist does. Recently, I had a close call with a family member who was fighting cancer, and it made me wonder how I might handle the death of a loved one. So, I created a phone number that I shared online and asked people to leave me a voicemail about a death they remember. I hoped the project would give me a greater appreciation for how diverse our experiences with death are, and thought, maybe, I could create some art out of the stories I collected.

Not surprisingly, the people who left me voicemails absolutely bared their souls. Some approached their grief with an awkward laugh, telling me how they were doing something embarrassing when they found out their loved one had died. Another person said, "I've never spoken to anybody about this . . ." But he couldn't go on and hung up.

LEARNING MORE ABOUT THE WORLD HELPS TO SPARK YOUR CURIOSITY.

There were so many heartbreaking messages; I even got one where a guy said, "I want to talk about my own death . . ." He explained he'd just been diagnosed with cancer and was quitting his job to spend time with his family. It was powerful stuff.

I never would have come up with the "Memories of Death" project without being curious about death, and then doing research to learn how other people experienced it. One thing I've noticed over the years is how learning something new often helps me expand my creative scope. Most creative people are innately curious, so if you can just keep pushing yourself to learn new stuff, I can pretty much guarantee it will keep your artistic juices flowing.

One word of caution here: if we get too obsessed with learning stuff, it can become another shiny ball—a reason to not create—because we may think that we don't know enough just yet to create masterful art. Stockpiling information is beneficial only to a

I had a friend who was a working disc jockey who said he'd pay me ten to fifteen dollars a joke and I thought holy shit, I could make a hundred dollars a week thinking up jokes, but I didn't know how to think of jokes. All I knew is if I thought of something, write it down. So I went to the library in Cleveland and got a book on how to write jokes.

- Drew Carey

certain point. Collecting too much information can cause creative paralysis. You'll keep growing your art skills if you can maintain an open mind and learn how to apply not only new materials but fresh approaches, techniques, and styles to your work.

And if you ever feel like you know everything, slow your roll a bit and try to bring yourself back to that novice mindset. Creativity is all about a cross-pollination of information and ideas. Learning more about the world gives us greater caches of information (as well as personal experiences) that we can use to create art, so learning about anything new (heck, even pre-Colonial candle making or the mating rituals of armadillos) could spark some creative ideas down the road.

9

Is Nothing Original?

You can find a ton of people online who love to shout, "Nothing is original anymore!" There are countless podcasts, TED Talks, and articles that coolly criticize how everything new today is actually not new, but a remix. Is that true, and if so . . . is that bad?

Recently, I spun myself into near madness trying to figure out what originality was. Looking at some of the popular new works in the world of art, literature, music, and film, I thought a lot of them seemed original at first. But if I looked a little closer, it also seemed possible to trace every hot new work back to something that came before it. I really wrapped my brain in a twist.

I even found myself questioning what I thought I was certain about in art. Was Michelangelo's famous sculpture *La Pietà* even original? When I researched it, I found that before him, multiple people had sculpted that exact scene before he did. More befuddling yet, I wondered if drawing itself was totally unoriginal—

since, when you think about it, Neanderthals had drawn on cave walls way before we Homo sapiens did. Was every drawing since the Ice Age just a derivative of those original cave drawings? Was my line of thinking totally insane? (Admittedly, it was.)

It finally dawned on me that the "everything is a remix" argument is true to a degree, but also relatively pointless. One big flaw in the theory is that most people who claim nothing is original anymore often use too broad of a categorization to make their case. They'll say things like, "This new sci-fi show is like Tolkien meets *Star Trek*. It's totally derivative." But they don't mention any of the elements that made the show different from its predecessors. They cherry-pick facts to make their argument while never acknowledging that, yes, there actually was a lot of new stuff going on in that show.

People love to look for the familiar in life. Our brains are wired to make these kinds of connections because it gives us a sense of certainty. If we see something new, we will immediately (and often subconsciously) try to categorize it by comparing it to things we've had exposure to in the past, which is one of the reasons we hear so many people arguing that nothing is original these days. Recently, I mentioned a flip-book I was working on to an acquaintance. He blurted in response: "I know an artistic duo that made a flip-book. But I guess everything's a remix, right?" I was a little surprised he dismissed my project as a hackneyed idea just because someone else had made a flip-book before, without even asking what I was planning to put inside the book. I started to contemplate the notion that the "nothing is original anymore" line has become its

WHAT WE VIEW AS ORIGINAL TODAY IS TOTALLY SUBJECTIVE.

own cliché. Have we all said it so many times that we've stopped looking for the one-of-a-kind elements in anything?

The truth is that what we view as original today is *totally subjective*, since it's based entirely on our individual experiences and perceptions. When we were kids, everything felt original because we had no frame of reference. Watching someone fart as they got their finger pulled always got a wild reaction. But by the time we grow up, we've already experienced a ton of stuff, so it's hard for anything to strike us as original. What may appear original to me may be old news to you, because we have a different knowledge base. That's why you might come across an art concept online that you've seen done before, and you'll still read comments below that gush, "Wow, genius!" Or "I can't believe no one thought of this before!" Even though you know it's not a new idea at all. Like beauty, talent, and humor . . . originality truly is in the eye of the beholder.

Nowadays, I feel like it's a total cliché to call someone else's idea unoriginal. You may even say it about your own ideas, so let me take you gently by the shoulders, shake you up, and tell you that just as creativity sucks, ORIGINALITY EXISTS! Don't dismiss your next idea just because it may have been done before, in one form or another. It's entirely possible to make something that looks similar to someone else's work, but our approach, our reasoning, and our tools for creating it could be totally different!

I've known many creative people who value originality as a primary goal in their careers, but I might also assert that these are the same colleagues who get the most frustrated. They view "pure originality" as what makes art valuable, but this is a feat that's also extremely difficult to achieve. Setting an unrealistic goal like this can cause some of us to stop creating art entirely. And the last thing any creative needs is another reason not to pursue our passions.

If originality is your main goal in creating, I say awesome. Getting there is as simple as looking at all the components in your work and noticing what's unique about it. However, if you want others to clearly see that you have discovered new land, it will be an interesting challenge. You're probably going to need to get a little weird (which, by the way, I always support). Try exploring your project systematically by taking one element and progressively pushing it further and further into the unknown. Do that, and you may even take your idea all the way to the extreme boundaries, which is where the rarified air of pure originality can be found in all art.

10

Once (okay, many times), someone asked me, "What inspires your work?" It's always a tough question for me to answer. I've never felt divinely inspired. Every idea I've conceived felt like it came from a very real, tangible place inside of me. Sure, things have sparked from here or there, but nothing with a capital "I" inspired. Though when I think back to when I was younger, I do remember getting the old "What inspires your work?" question frequently. So much so that for a while I sought out inspiration. It felt like something I was supposed to look for. And I was confused when I didn't find much.

I've met many people who talk of inspiration in this necessary way: "I'm waiting to be inspired before I create again." Or "I'm making the extra bedroom into a studio so I'll be ready when inspiration strikes." *Whaaa?* I've struggled with this because if my goal is producing work, then I don't want to get held up waiting for anything. Lately I've begun to say: screw this whole inspiration thing. I don't want to need any outside influence to inspire me to create. I just want to create what feels right to me, right now.

For people who don't have a creative passion, the idea that artists would need inspiration to create something seems necessary because they've been taught by society that artists are always inspired by something. But it's not true. Most creatives tend to just make stuff and come up with the reasoning or inspiration for the work later on. Inspiration can be a beautiful and powerful thing, but if we expect inspiration to be a driving force behind our art, we may be waiting a long, long time! Waiting for inspiration is a game that's not rigged in your favor.

WAITING FOR INSPIRATION IS A GAME THAT'S NOT RIGGED IN YOUR FAVOR.

Besides, do you really want to put your art career in the hands of an unreliable world? Heck no. Even though I totally understand wanting to be *inspired by something*, please know you can create amazing work without inspiration. In fact, you should. Even if this sounds really insular: never rely on something outside of yourself to get you going. The best way to come up with new ideas is to get curious about something. This puts the onus on you, rather than on the outside world, to do it. Stoking your natural curiosity will help you push through to keep your creative fire burning. If you're looking for inspiration and finding an empty void, then you may need to chat with your creative buddy to help you remember why you do this and why you love this, or take a step back because you're putting too much pressure on yourself and need a break. It may also be helpful to look at different ways you can give yourself a mental shake so you feel fresh again. Turn your focus from inspiration to internal curiosity. Then go do your thing.

I like to take the small things and make them big, and I like to take the big things like disease and death and make them small.

- Larry David

11

The Sendoff

As you venture forth in your creative life, you'll find that moment in every stage when all the hard work comes together to deliver an idea to you. All that development and patience practiced in hope that something will come of it? *That*'s the magic. The quest you're on is to find that next idea—the one you can't wait to have time to execute, relying on what you do know to make it happen and relying on what you don't know to give you that vast margin of space to trust the learning process and know that it never ends.

We all come to this work for different reasons, and each of us experiences the glory of it from our own unique angles. Some of us bask in the freedom to create, some desire recognition, and some just want the paycheck. Some of us just live for the times we can spend the entire day alone working on a project and others love extended collaboration with a group. But if there's one thing that we have in common, it's that we keep showing up to our art. Even on the dry days, this is what nourishes the artist's spirit more than anything. So, grab the hand of your creative buddy, look for your own curiosity, have lots of shitty ideas, crush your idols, get lucky, and be a little crazy. Why not? It's your creative life.

NOTES

Page 5 Marc Maron. "Episode 916: Mary Steenburgen." *WTF with Marc Maron*. Podcast audio. May 17, 2018. http://www.wtfpod.com/podcast /episode-916-mary-steenburgen.

Page 7 David Joel. *Monet at Vetheuil and on the Norman Coast, 1878–1883*. Woodbridge, UK: Antique Collectors' Club, 2002, 70.

Page 17 Michael Ian Black. "Audio Story 92: Jay and Mark Duplass." *How to Be Amazing with Michael Ian Black*. Podcast audio. August 22, 2018. https:// beta.prx.org/stories/252062.

Page 19 Michael Ian Black. "Audio Story 85: Nell Scovell." *How to Be Amazing with Michael Ian Black*. Podcast audio. May 16, 2018. https://beta .prx.org/stories/243618.

Page 30 Kurt Andersen. "Richard Russo and Jenny Boylan on Plot Twists in Books—and Life." *Studio 360*. Podcast audio. May 19, 2016. https://www .wnyc.org/story/richard-russo-jenny-boylan-everybodys-fool/.

Page 42 Terry Gross. "'Mad Max' Director George Miller: The Audience Tells You 'What Your Film Is.'" *Fresh Air*. Podcast audio. February 8, 2016.

https://www.npr.org/programs/fresh-air/2016/02/08/466020911/fresh
-air-for-february-8-2016.

Page 55   Mike Sacks. "Interview: Tom Scharpling." In *Poking a Dead Frog*
(New York: Penguin, 2014), 286.

Page 75   Ian Bonhote, dir. *McQueen*. 2018; United Kingdom: Misfits
Entertainment and Salon Pictures. Digital video.

Page 76   Marc Maron. "Episode 915: Josh Brolin." *WTF with Marc Maron*.
Podcast audio. May 14, 2018. https://www.wtfpod.com/podcast/episode
-915-josh-brolin.

Page 94   Krista Tippett. "David Whyte: The Conversational Nature of
Reality." *On Being*. Podcast audio. April 7, 2016. https://onbeing.org
/programs/david-whyte-the-conversational-nature-of-reality/.

Page 120   Marc Maron. "Episode 693: Ethan Hawke." *WTF with Marc Maron*.
Podcast audio. March 28, 2016. http://www.wtfpod.com/podcast/episodes
/episode_693_-_ethan_hawke.

Page 141   Elizabeth Gilbert. *Big Magic*. New York: Penguin, 2015, 189.

Page 166   Michael Ian Black. "Audio Story 26: Chuck Klosterman." *How to Be
Amazing with Michael Ian Black*. Podcast audio. March 16, 2016. https://
beta.prx.org/stories/174446.

Page 175   Marc Maron. "Episode 912: Drew Carey." *WTF with Marc Maron*.
Podcast audio. May 3, 2018. http://www.wtfpod.com/podcast/episode-912
-drew-carey.

Page 183   David Remnick. "Episode 24: Larry David, Amy Poehler, and Randy
Newman." *The New Yorker Radio Hour*. Podcast audio. April 1, 2016. https://
www.newyorker.com/podcast/the-new-yorker-radio-hour/episode-24
-larry-david-amy-poehler-and-randy-newman.

WHOA! I'M ACTUALLY DONE WITH THE BOOK. I GUESS IT'S BACK TO ARTIN'!

LATER

I JUST WANT TO MAKE THIS PROJECT THAT I'VE BEEN PLANNING FOR THE LAST MONTH BUT I DON'T HAVE THE MONEY.... THIS SUCKS.

SUCKS HUH?

YAH. ... WHAT. YOU THINK I SHOULD TAKE MY OWN ADVICE?

HOWEVER YOU INTERPRET IT.

6 MONTHS LATER

HOW WAS YOUR DAY?

IT WAS GOOD. I APPLIED FOR A LOAN FOR 10 GRAND TO MAKE ART.

WHAT?!

I'M GETTING CREATIVE WITH MONEY. GONNA USE A LOT AND SPEND NONE. I'LL MAKE A PIC WITH THE CASH. THEN PUT IT ALL BACK IN THE BANK AND PAY OFF THE LOAN WITH THE SAME MONEY I TOOK OUT.

YOU'RE CRAZY. THINK THEY'LL APPROVE IT?

DOUBTFUL.